Non-Chew Cookbook

GW01548339

By J. Randy Wilson

Foreword by
Mark A. Piper, D.M.D., M.D.

ISBN 0-9616299-0-8

Fourth Edition
© Copyright 1985 J. Randy Wilson

To my wonderful wife, Bobbie,
who has inspired me throughout my adult life.

PREFACE

I hope you enjoy the recipes as much as I have enjoyed compiling this cookbook. It is my pleasure to share with you a new world of cooking and dining pleasure that is delightful for the entire family.

I have tried to provide you with recipes and hints that I hope are helpful to those on a soft food diet. Perhaps you have your own favorite recipe or helpful hint, and I invite you to share those with me. As I learn of new ideas and recipes, I will include them in future revisions of this book. A newsletter may also develop. Please complete the card found in the back of this book and mail today. I will add your name to the mailing list for future recipes and hints.

Good nutrition is very important for all of us. We keep asking ourselves what should we eat to maintain good health. The following dietary guidelines form a basis for good eating habits.

1. Eat a variety of foods.
2. Maintain ideal weight.
3. Avoid too much fat, saturated fat, and cholesterol.
4. Eat foods with adequate starch and fiber.
5. Avoid too much sugar.
6. Avoid too much sodium.
7. If you drink alcohol, do so in moderation.

For those on a restricted sodium diet, I have eliminated salt where it does not dramatically enhance the flavor. When a recipe calls for salt, you may wish to omit the salt if your diet requires restricted sodium intake.

I have included for you the nutritional analysis for each serving of all the recipes included in this book. This will help you determine how the recipe contributes to overall nutrition. This was made possible by the Nutri-Fit computer program at Colorado State University, Department of Food Science and Human Nutrition, Extension Service.

The recipes contained in this book may teach you new and creative ways to prepare food for the person on a soft food diet. These can, however, be enjoyed by the rest of the family. Delightful and nutritious recipes make eating enjoyable and good health attainable. I urge you to be creative with your daily diet.

I wish you the best of health and happy eating.

J. Randy Wilson

ACKNOWLEDGEMENTS AND CREDITS

I would like to give a special thanks to the following people who assisted me in this book. They gave their time, professional advice and recipes.

Mark A. Piper, D.M.D., M.D., P.A.
St. Petersburg, Florida

Peter E. Dawson, D.D.S.
St. Petersburg, Florida

Jennifer Anderson, M.S., R.D.
Food and Nutrition Extension Specialist
Colorado State University
Fort Collins, Colorado

James D. Cummins, D.D.S.
Glenwood Springs, Colorado

Ken Wiencek, D.D.S.
Glenwood Springs, Colorado

Cheryl Wright, R.N.
Glenwood Springs, Colorado

Bonnie Sherman, Home Economist
Glenwood Springs, Colorado

Debra Mestas, R.D.
Glenwood Springs, Colorado

Maggie Klink
Glenwood Springs, Colorado

Phyllis Hackett, R.N.
Glenwood Springs, Colorado

John Powers
New York, New York

FOREWORD

by Mark A. Piper, D.M.D., M.D.

The greatest pleasure that a cookbook can offer is a palatable selection of appetizers, soups, salads, vegetables, entrees and desserts that will fulfill our needs for gustatory enjoyment. To this end, this book certainly meets the requirements of any good cookbook. However, in satisfying the special demands of a large number of people, the inception and goals of this cookbook are to offer nutritionally balanced and tasteful recipes to individuals whose choice of foods is limited by their ability to chew.

Millions of Americans suffer from the consequences of poor chewing function. For many, this has been the result of birth deformity, and for others the loss of chewing ability has been secondary to facial trauma or surgical alteration. Given the limitation of abnormal mastication, these individuals find little to rejoice in most cookbooks.

The number of people in the United States with loss of chewing function is enormous. Malformations of the facial skeleton, with significant alteration in the structures of the bite complex, occur in approximately five out of every one hundred births. More serious facial deformities and clefts of the facial bones occur in one out of every six hundred births. These individuals, if uncorrected surgically and orthodontically, face a lifetime of nutritional compromise because of their inability to masticate common foods. For these people, the attempt at proper dietary intake may be a difficult, if not impossible, task to undertake.

Edentulous people form the largest group with permanent compromise in chewing ability. Twenty-five million Americans have lost their teeth due to dental caries and periodontal disease. The more fortunate ones are fitted with prosthetic teeth that offer an adequate replacement for the lost natural dentition. The remainder, however, either cannot be fitted with dentures or cannot afford reconstructive surgery and dentistry that is now available to rebuild the mouth structures. When faced with the loss of a function that was once enjoyed daily, and perhaps taken for granted, these people not only lose the ability to eat certain foods, but also may deprive themselves of the will to gain adequate nutrition because of psychological depression associated with the lost function.

Another major nutritional public health problem is found in persons with malignancies. Cancer of the mouth is discovered each year in 60,000 Americans. Care of this dreadful menace may force the surgeon to ablate major structures of the mouth, facial skeleton, or neck. Heroic reconstruction techniques may restore normal appearance for a fraction of these individuals. However, whether reconstructed or not, the ability to chew is reduced, and if nutrition is not maintained, life expectancy can be further compromised.

Other groups also bear the burden of decreased chewing function. Headache sufferers, similar to the spouse of the author of this cookbook, may suffer years of chronic headache and facial pain secondary to bite problems and disorders of the temporomandibular joints. This debilitating pain, found 90% of the time in young females, may be misdiagnosed for years as migraines, tension headaches, or pre-menstrual syndrome. The frustration faced by many of these individuals as they seek one physician after another eventually leads to a resolution to live with the pain. If left undiagnosed, most temporomandibular joint or TMJ patients will discover that much of their headache pain relates directly to the chewing of coarse food. An alteration to a softer diet therefore becomes necessary. For those who are fortuitous enough to be diagnosed, the specialist may prescribe a soft or "non-chewing" diet as a part of the surgical or non-surgical correction of the problem.

Tens of millions of other Americans have temporary loss of mastication each year. This may be the result of minor oral surgery, reconstructive jaw surgery, or infections of the mouth. The serious consequences of acquired malnutrition are usually not seen in this group of patients. However, adequate nutritional intake to ensure proper healing is a necessity, even when limited chewing may be present for only a few days.

When most cookbooks are consulted, emphasis is placed on the actual taste of the food. For people with no restrictions on food texture, the usual recipes serve their needs for entertainment or celebration of special events. When the person with altered chewing function uses such a cookbook, there is usually disappointment with both the variety of foods available to them as well as with the nutritional content contained in these more limited recipes. The good food that most of us take for granted has become for them a burden to chew or swallow. Selections may become narrowed to those items that are easiest to eat or most convenient. As the variety of foods decreases, necessary nutrients are no longer attained, and proper nutrition suffers. This in turn may lead to the consequences of malnutrition and undernutrition including disability, disease, poor healing, and mental anguish.

Because of a decrease in food choices, those individuals on a liquid or soft diet must have a basic understanding of nutrition. As a science, proper nutrition should supply adequate calories, minerals, vitamins and water. Protein, carbohydrates and fat provide the calories necessary for the energy requirements of the body. Depending upon the sex, body build, surgical status and activity level, more or less caloric intake may be required. Minerals and vitamins provide no calories, but they are essential in maintaining the metabolic processes of the body. Minerals are important components of body tissues, blood, iron, and bone calcium. Both minerals and vitamins function in the utilization of energy and in the building and healing of body tissues. Water makes up about 70% of the total body weight ard it is important in absorption of nutrients and in the elimination of waste products.

In determining how we can best balance calories, vitamins, and minerals, nutritional allowances have been developed by the Food and Nutrition Board of the National Academy of Sciences -National Research Council. The Food and Nutrition Board has formulated "Recommended Dietary Allowances" to guide daily nutrient intake for maintenance of gocd nutrition for the general population of the United States. A table of these recommended dietary allowances is included in the Nutrition Chapter of the book. These allowances are only references, and actual individual needs based upon starting nutritional status and special metabolic requirements such as surgery must be considered. Some individual variations may occur, and therefore, any nutritional requirements above the RDA should be prescribed by a properly trained physician or nutritionist.

Caloric intake tables are also included in the Nutrition Chapter. These are based upon the caloric requirements to maintain a normal body weight in a person free of disease processes. Caloric requirements may increase in disease or surgery and they may decrease in more sedentary lifestyle. Therefore, caloric recommendations may depend upon the actual status of the individual.

Proper nutrition is an important factor in health and disease. There are no geographic or socio-economic barriers to many of the millions of Americans with compromised chewing capacity, and it is this group that is more likely to suffer nutritional debility. This book addresses both the nutritional as well as the gustatory requirements of the individual on a soft or liquid diet. It is hoped that it will stimulate the palates of those who otherwise are bored by their chewing restrictions and at the same time, improve or maintain the nutrition important for good health and recovery from surgery and disease.

BASIC NUTRITION

by Debra Mestas, R.D.

With the ever increasing awareness of health and fitness, more people are realizing the importance of food in maintenance of good health in the normal person, and in the recovery of an ill person. Nutrition is basically the food you eat and how your body uses it for growth, activity, reproduction, lactation, and health maintenance. Good nutrition means there is adequate energy for tissue growth and repair, prevention of deficiency diseases, and resistance to disease and infections.

There are six nutrients supplied in food. These are water, protein, fat, carbohydrates, vitamins, and minerals. Protein, fat, and carbohydrates are the three that provide calories, which is the amount of energy fuel in the food. There are Recommended Dietary Allowances (R.D.A.) established by the Food and Nutrition Board of the National Research Council for protein, vitamins, minerals and calories.

Water is absolutely necessary to life, and it is found in all body cells, and accounts for two-thirds of total body weight. Water helps the dissolving and digestion of food and in the elimination of waste products. It is found in all beverages and in many solid foods.

Protein provides amino acids which are the building blocks for all body cells, hormones, and enzymes. It is essential for growth and repair. Complete proteins contain all eight essential amino acids and are found in meat, poultry, fish, dairy products, and eggs. Incomplete proteins do not have the essential amino acids in sufficient amounts and are found in plant products like dried beans and peas, grains, and cereals. By including incomplete proteins in the diet, one can decrease amounts of animal protein needed.

Fats provide calories and essential fatty acids necessary for healthy tissues. Fats take longer to digest so they help achieve a "full" feeling after a meal. Fats are found in oils, butters, salad dressings, meats, and dairy foods.

Carbohydrates supply energy in the form of simple sugars and complex starches, and also furnish bulk in the form of dietary fiber. We need enough carbohydrate to supply heat and energy so that our protein will not have to be diverted to meet energy demands. It is found in cereals, grains, potatoes, fruits, vegetables, honey, and sugars.

Vitamins are needed for healthy body processes and proper metabolism of other nutrients. Vitamins A, D, E, K are fat-soluble so are not excreted from the body via urine. A and D can build up to toxic levels and cause dangerous side effects. Caution should be taken when vitamin A and D supplements are used.

Water soluble vitamins include the B-complex vitamins and vitamin C. These vitamins aren't stored in the body and are excreted in the urine if daily needs are exceeded. Mega-doses of these do have some possible side-effects. Vitamins are found in foods in a balanced diet and in vitamin-enriched foods. If illness or poor eating habits are present, a multi-vitamin may benefit. It should be emphasized that supplemental vitamins can be a waste of effect and money, and be harmful if taken in excess. Synthetic vitamins are used by the body the same as "natural" ones with the possible exception of vitamin E.

Minerals are needed for building body structures, tissues, and regulating body processes. Calcium, phosphorus, sodium, potassium, magnesium and sulfur are needed in large amounts. Other "trace" minerals like iron, copper, zinc and fluorine are needed in small amounts. Minerals can be harmful if too much is taken. Minerals are found in dairy products, protein foods, whole grain foods, and dark leafy vegetables. An iron supplement can benefit menstruating and pregnant women, and growing children because their higher needs are often not met.

A balanced diet normally supplies enough nutrients for daily needs plus some extra. It is recommended that daily menu plans are made using the Basic Four Food Groups as the backbone. For adults the suggested amounts are:

> Milk — 2 or more cups/day with cheese, ice cream as substitute for part.
> Meat — 2 or more 4 oz. servings/day.

Fruits/Vegetables — 2 or more ½ c. servings of each/day.

Breads/Cereals — 4 or more servings/day.

It is very important to eat a variety of foods to insure adequate nutrient intake. Normal growth patterns and a desireable weight should be maintained. It is also recommended that salt, fats, cholesterol, simple sugars and "empty calorie" foods be decreased and fresh fruits and vegetables be increased.

Swallowing/Chewing Problems

When swallowing or chewing is made difficult by oral surgery, poor-fitting dentures, cancer therapy, or gum disease it is easy to get into a habit of limiting food selections. An inadequate diet often occurs in these situations. Some helpful hints include:

1. Cutting or grinding food into appropriate size pieces, and putting into a cream sauce or mixing with other foods as in a casserole.
2. Making rich soups of creamed or blended meats and vegetables or dried beans, peas, lentils, soybeans, etc.

3. Adding eggs and cheeses to increase protein.
4. Using mashed or pureed fruits and vegetables or their juices.
5. Cooking hot cereals in milk instead of water.
6. Using gelatins, ice creams, puddings, custards, milk shakes.

Boosting Protein
1. Add dry skim milk powder to regular milk, sauces gravies, puddings. Add extra ice-cream to shakes and half-and-half or evaporated milk in instant cocoa, soups, or puddings.
3. Add grated cheeses to casseroles, vegetables, sauces. Blended cottage cheese makes a great dip.
4. Finely chopped eggs can be added to sauces, casseroles, meat salads. Make beverages and desserts that use eggs like eggnogs, angel food cake.
5. Add chopped or pureed meats to soups and casseroles.

Boosting Calories
1. Melt margarine onto hot toast, cereals, vegetables, rice, eggs.
2. Use sour cream on potatoes, meats, fruits.
3. Use cream cheese on breads, fruit.
4. Use mayonnaise instead of salad dressings.
5. Put peanut butter on apples, bananas, celery, carrots, breads.
6. Top puddings, pies, hot chocolate, gelatin, and fruit with whipped cream.
7. Use honey, candies, jelly, but only after eating nutritious foods if possible!

Boosting Fiber
1. Use whole grain breads and cereals.
2. Use unpeeled apples and potatoes.
3. Eat oranges and grapefruit and their unstrained juices.
4. Add sunflower, sesame, poppy, or pumpkin seeds to salads, breads, etc.
5. Make soups with dried beans, peas, lentils, soybeans, etc.
6. Add dates, raisins, figs, dried apricots to hot cereals, cakes, etc.
7. Make carrot or cabbage slaw with pineapple and raisins.
8. Add broccoli, cauliflower, corn to soups, casseroles.
9. Top sandwiches and salads with alfalfa or bean sprouts.
10. Use more tomatoes in sauces, soups, as well as sliced.
11. Snack on popcorn.
12. Add fresh parsley to salads.

Recommended Reading

A Handbook of Commonsense Nutrition.
Williams, S. R. C. V. Mosby Co., 1983.

Nutrition Handbook, 3rd Edition.
Nasset, E. S. Harper & Row 1982.

Food, Nutrition, and Diet Therapy.
Krause and Mahan. W. B. Saunders Co. 1979.

Quick Reference to Clinical Nutrition.
Halpern, S. L. J. B. Lippincott Co. 1979.

Nutrition for Patients Receiving Chemotherapy and Radiation Treatment.
American Cancer Society Inc., 1974.

HINTS
AND
FOOD GROUPS

Atmosphere makes a difference: An attractively set table with flowers or other such items, can make the meal more enjoyable. Eating with friends, having music at dinner time, and varying the place in your house where you eat are suggested.

Make-up own recipes: Try ice cream mixed with ginger ale or your favorite carbonated beverage as a drink. Try a milkshake, frozen yogurt or eggnog.

Eat small meals more often.

Vary the color of foods served: Arrange food attractively. Add garnishes such as an orange slice, a slice of tomato or a sprig of parsley.

Use a blender or food processor: If you like vegetable soup, for example, heat then blend it. Food tastes better if it is cooked before it is blended. It is easier to blend warm food. Cut meat up in small pieces and add gravy to them prior to blending.

Many soft foods: Such as mashed potatoes, yogurt, scrambled eggs, poached eggs, egg custards, milkshakes, puddings, gelatins, creamy cereals and ice cream.

Try tilting your head back or moving it forward to make swallowing easier.

Rinse your mouth: To remove debris, to stimulate your gums, to lubricate your mouth or to put a fresh taste in your mouth.

Craving foods: If these foods can not be blended, you can place in mouth to savor the flavor and eliminate desire.

Vegetables: Most vegetables, if well cooked, can be served whole, and each bite can be mashed with fork before eating. This is much more appetizing.

Spice up baby food with seasonings.

Beverages: All types of beverages.

Bread and cereal products: Blended or strained cooked cereal such as cream of wheat, farina, hominy grits, strained oatmeal, wheat cream meal; macaroni or spaghetti; noodles; rice. Make sure enough liquid is added for smooth consistency. Bran can be added to many foods to increase fiber.

Meat, fowl, fish, eggs, cheese: Blended or strained beef, lamb, pork, veal, fowl, liver; eggs prepared in any way but fried or hard boiled; small curd cottage cheese; prepared "junior" baby food.

Milk and milk products: All milk and milk products, such as ice cream, custards and yogurt.

Fruits: All fruit juices and nectars; fresh canned or cooked fruit, such as peaches, pears, apples, apricots, bananas and cherries; prepared "junior" baby foods. All fruits should be cooked before blending. Very ripe fruits will blend best.

Vegetables: All vegetable juices such as V-8, carrot, celery and tomato; cooked, mild flavored pureed vegetables such as asparagus, beans (green and wax), beets, carrots, peas, spinach, winter squash; tomato puree in combination with other foods; mashed white potatoes; prepared "junior" baby foods.

Soups: All meat broths; all cream soups prepared with mashed potatoes, pureed vegetables, or strained meat.

Sweets and desserts: All smooth textured desserts such as custards, gelatin, ice cream, puddings, rennet desserts; ovaltine; jelly; sherbet; sugar; syrups (chocolate, butterscotch, caramel, marshmallow).

Fats: Butter, cream, margarine, vegetable fats and oils.

Condiments, spices, sauces, specialties: Salt and spice. Catsup, mustard, steak sauce, chili powder, vinegar, pepper, etc.

Commercial products: Meritene (powder or liquid); Sustagen, Metrecal, Instant Breakfast, Gevral, Sego, Sustacal (liquid or powder), Provimalt, and prepared "junior" baby foods.

Major Nutrients
Their Functions and Food Sources

Nutrient	Function in the Body	Food Sources
Protein	Basic building block of all tissues. Builds and repairs all body tissues. Supplies energy. Helps form antibodies, which fight infection.	Meat, fish, poultry, eggs, milk, cheese, dried peas and beans, soybeans, nuts, cereals breads.
Carbohydrate	Supplies energy for heat and mechanical work.	Sugars, fruits, vegetables, cereals, breads, rice, pasta.
Fat	Supplies energy to do physical work. Major storage form of excess energy in the body. Aids in absorption of vitamins A, D, E, and K and Calcium.	Margarine, vegetable oils, butter, salad dressings, fatty meats, whole milk products, egg yolks, nuts, cheese, bacon, shortening, lard.
Vitamin A	Promotes normal vision in dim light. Promotes healthy skin and tissue lining. Helps maintain resistance to infection.	Liver, eggs, dark green and yellow vegetables, butter, margarine, peaches, cantaloupe, apricots, whole milk products, low-fat milk with vitamin A added, fish liver oils.
Thiamin or Vitamin B_1	Promotes normal digestion, growth, and appetite. Helps keep the nervous system healthy. Helps change food into energy.	Pork; liver; heart; kidney; dried peas and beans; nuts; wheat germ; whole-grain, restored, enriched, and fortified cereals and breads.
Riboflavin or Vitamin B_2	Necessary for the release of energy from food. Helps keep eyes, mouth, and skin healthy. Promotes vitality and growth.	Beef, pork, lamb, liver, milk and milk products, yogurt, eggs, green leafy vegetables, cheese, peanuts, enriched and fortified cereals and breads.

Nutrient	Function in the Body	Food Sources
Niacin	Helps keep skin, mouth, and nervous system healthy. Helps convert food into energy. Aids in digestion.	Lean meat; fish; poultry; liver; kidney; peanuts; peanut butter; mushrooms; dried peas and beans; whole-grain restored, enriched, and fortified cereals and breads
Vitamin B_6	Aids in digestion of protein.	Meat, fish, chicken, liver, egg yolks, peanuts, peanut butter, bananas, potatoes, corn, whole-grain and fortified cereals and breads.
Vitamin B_{12}	Necessary for proper functioning of all cells.	Meat, fish, liver, kidney, eggs, milk, cheese.
Folic acid (folacin)	Necessary for the formation of blood cells.	Liver, dried beans, peanuts, walnuts, filberts, dark green vegetables.
Vitamin C or ascorbic acid	Important for healthy tissues: gums, blood vessels, bones, and teeth. Helps promote healing, stamina, and energy.	Citrus fruits and juices, strawberries, cantaloupe, broccoli, cabbage, tomatoes, tomato juice, green peppers, potatoes, leafy greens, watermelon, brussel sprouts.
Vitamin D	Aids in absorption of calcium and phosphorus, which build and maintain bones and teeth.	Fish liver oils, fortified milk, liver, egg yolks, herring, mackerel, canned salmon, sardines, sunshine.
Vitamin E	Important for the stability of substances in the body tissues.	Liver, eggs, whole-grain cereals and breads, whole milk, margarine, salad oil, salad dressing, green leafy vegetables.

Nutrient	Function in the Body	Food Sources
Calcium	Needed to build bones and teeth. Helps nerves, muscles, and heart function properly. Helps blood clotting.	Milk and milk products, salmon, sardines, green leafy vegetables.
Iron	Helps build red blood cells.	Meat; liver; egg yolks; tuna; oysters; green leafy vegetables; dried fruits; whole-grain, restored, enriched, and fortified cereals and breads.
Phosphorus	Needed to build bones and teeth.	Meat, fish, poultry, eggs, dried beans, peanuts, whole-grain cereals and breads, milk and milk products.
Magnesium	Needed for proper functioning of body cells.	Dried beans, nuts, dark green vegetables, whole-grain cereals and breads.
Iodine	Needed to help regulate many body functions.	Iodized salt, seafood.

DESIRABLE WEIGHTS

(for adults 25 years and older)

Weight in Pounds According to Frame
(in indoor clothing)

WOMEN

Height
(with shoes on)
2-inch heels

Feet	Inches	Small Frame	Medium Frame	Large Frame
4	10	92- 98	96-107	104-119
4	11	94-101	98-110	106-122
5	0	96-104	101-113	109-125
5	1	99-107	104-116	112-128
5	2	102-110	107-119	115-131
5	3	105-113	110-122	118-134
5	4	108-116	113-126	121-138
5	5	111-119	116-130	125-142
5	6	114-123	120-135	129-146
5	7	118-127	124-139	133-150
5	8	122-131	128-143	137-154
5	9	126-135	132-147	141-158
5	10	130-140	136-151	145-163
5	11	134-144	140-150	149-168
6	0	138-148	144-159	153-173

For girls between 18 and 25, subtract 1 pound for each year under 25.

Courtesy of Metropolitan Life Insurance Company

DESIRABLE WEIGHTS

(for adults 25 years and older)

Weight in Pounds According to Frame

(in indoor clothing)

MEN

Height
(with shoes on)
1-inch heels

Feet	Inches	Small Frame	Medium Frame	Large Frame
5	2	112-120	118-129	126-141
5	3	115-123	121-133	129-144
5	4	118-126	124-136	132-148
5	5	121-129	127-139	135-152
5	6	124-133	130-143	138-156
5	7	128-137	134-147	142-161
5	8	132-141	138-152	147-166
5	9	136-145	142-156	151-170
5	10	140-150	146-160	155-174
5	11	144-154	150-165	159-179
6	0	148-158	154-170	164-184
6	1	152-162	158-175	168-189
6	2	156-167	162-180	173-194
6	3	160-171	167-185	178-199
6	4	164-175	172-190	182-204

Courtesy of Metropolitan Life Insurance Company

Recommended Dietary Allowances 1980 *

Age years	Weight kg	Weight lbs	Height cm	Height in	Protein g	Fat-Soluble Vitamins Vitamin A RE	Vitamin D µg	Vitamin E mg	Water-Soluble Vitamins Vitamin C mg	Thiamin mg	Riboflavin mg	Niacin mg equiv	Vitamin B6 mg	Folacin µg	Vitamin B12 µg	Minerals Calcium mg	Phosphorous mg	Magnesium mg	Iron mg	Zinc mg	Iodine µg
Infants																					
0.0-0.5	6	13	60	24	kgx2.2	420	10	3	35	0.3	0.4	6	0.3	30	0.5	360	240	50	10	3	40
0.5-1.0	9	20	71	28	kgx2.2	400	10	4	35	0.5	0.6	8	0.6	45	1.5	540	360	70	15	5	50
Children																					
1-3	13	29	90	35	23	400	10	5	45	0.7	0.8	9	0.9	100	2.0	800	800	150	15	10	70
4-6	20	44	112	44	30	500	10	6	45	0.9	1.0	11	1.3	200	2.5	800	800	200	10	10	90
7-10	28	62	132	52	34	700	10	7	45	1.2	1.4	16	1.6	300	3.0	800	800	250	10	10	120
Males																					
11-14	45	99	157	62	45	1000	10	8	50	1.4	1.6	18	1.8	400	3.0	1200	1200	350	18	15	150
15-18	66	145	176	69	58	1000	10	10	60	1.4	1.7	18	2.0	400	3.0	1200	1200	400	18	15	150
19-22	70	154	178	70	58	1000	7.5	10	60	1.5	1.7	19	2.2	400	3.0	800	800	350	10	15	150
23-50	70	154	178	70	58	1000	5	10	60	1.4	1.6	18	2.2	400	3.0	800	800	350	10	15	150
51+	70	154	178	70	58	1000	5	10	60	1.2	1.4	16	2.2	400	3.0	800	800	350	10	15	150
Females																					
11-14	46	101	157	62	46	800	10	8	50	1.1	1.3	15	1.8	400	3.0	1200	1200	300	18	15	150
15-18	55	120	163	64	46	800	10	8	60	1.1	1.3	14	2.0	400	3.0	1200	1200	300	18	15	150
19-22	55	120	163	64	44	800	7.5	8	60	1.1	1.3	14	2.0	400	3.0	800	800	300	18	15	150
23-50	55	120	163	64	44	800	5	8	60	1.0	1.2	13	2.0	400	3.0	800	800	300	18	15	150
51+	55	120	163	64	44	800	5	8	60	1.0	1.2	13	2.0	400	3.0	800	800	300	10	15	150
Pregnant					+30	+200	+5	+2	+20	+0.4	+0.3	+2	+0.6	+400	+1.0	+400	+400	+150	**	+5	+25
Lactating					+20	+400	+5	+3	+40	+0.5	+0.5	+5	+0.5	+100	+1.0	+400	+400	+150	**	+10	+50

The allowances are intended to provide for individual variation among most normal, healthy people in the United States under usual environmental stresses. They were designed for the maintenance of good nutrition. Diets should be based on a variety of common foods in order to provide other nutrients for which human requirements have been less well defined. *From *Recommended Dietary Allowances*, 9th edition, 1980, National Academy of Sciences, Washington, D.C.

**Supplemental iron is recommended.

Mean Heights & Weights And Recommended Caloric Intake*

age and sex group	weight kg	weight lb	height cm	height in	energy needs MJ	energy needs kcal	energy range in kcal
Infants							
0.0-0.5 yr.	6	13	60	24	kg × 0.48	kg × 115	95-145
0.5-1.0 yr.	9	20	71	28	kg × 0.44	kg × 105	80-135
Children							
1-3 yr.	13	29	90	35	5.5	1,300	900-1,800
4-6 yr.	20	44	112	44	7.1	1,700	1,300-2,300
7-10 yr.	28	62	132	52	10.1	2,400	1,650-3,300
Males							
11-14 yr.	45	99	157	62	11.3	2,700	2,000-3,700
15-18 yr.	66	145	176	69	11.8	2,800	2,100-3,900
19-22 yr.	70	154	177	70	12.2	2,900	2,500-3,300
23-50 yr.	70	154	178	70	11.3	2,700	2,300-3,100
51-75 yr.	70	154	178	70	10.1	2,400	2,000-2,800
76+ yr.	70	154	178	70	8.6	2,050	1,650-2,450
Females							
11-14 yr.	46	101	157	62	9.2	2,200	1,500-3,000
15-18 yr.	55	120	163	64	8.8	2,100	1,200-3,000
19-22 yr.	55	120	163	64	8.8	2,100	1,700-2,500
23-50 yr.	55	120	163	64	8.4	2,000	1,600-2,400
51-75 yr.	55	120	163	64	7.6	1,800	1,400-2,200
76+ yr.	55	120	163	64	6.7	1,600	1,200-2,000
Pregnancy						+ 300	
Lactation						+ 500	

*From Recommended Dietary Allowances, Revised 1980, Food and Nutrition Board, National Academy of Sciences - National Research Council, Washington, D.C. The data in this table have been assembled from the observed median heights and weights of children, together with desirable weights for adults for mean heights of men (70 in.) and women (64 in.) between the ages of eighteen and thirty-four as surveyed in the U. S. population (DHEW/NCHS data).

Energy allowances for the young adults are for men and women doing light work. The allowances for the two older age groups represent mean energy needs over these age spans, allowing for a 2 percent decrease in basal (resting) metabolic rate per decade and a reduction in activity of 200 kcal per day for men and women between fifty-one and seventy-five years; 500 kcal for men over seventy-five years; and 400 kcal for women over seventy-five. The customary range of daily energy output is shown for adults in the range column and is based on a variation in energy needs of ± 400 kcal at any one age, emphasizing the wide range of energy intakes appropriate for any group of people.

Energy allowances for children through age eighteen are based on median energy intakes of children of these ages followed in longitudinal growth studies. Ranges are the 10th and 90th percentiles of energy intake, to indicate range of energy consumption among children in these ages. (*From* Recommended Dietary Allowances, Ninth Revised Edition, 1980.)

Limeade

½   cup fresh-squeezed lime juice
1½ cups club soda
4   packets of Equal®

Mix together and chill. Serve over ice cubes. Makes 1 serving.

Nutritional Analysis Per Serving:

Calories: 47	Vitamin C: . . . . .26 mg
Protein: . . . . .0 g	Thiamine: . . . . .0 mg
Carbohydrates: . . . . .15 g	Riboflavin: . . . . .0 mg
Fat: . . . . .0 g	Niacin: . . . . .1 mg
Phosphate: . . . . .13 mg	Calcium: . . . . .11 mg
Potassium: . . . . .128 mg	Iron: . . . . .3 mg
Zinc: . . . . .0 mg	Cholesterol: . . . . .0 mg
Vitamin A: . . . . .12 iu	Sodium: . . . . .1 mg

Old-Fashioned Lemonade

1   cup fresh lemon juice
15 packets of Equal®
4   cups cold water
1   lemon, sliced

Combine the lemon juice and Equal® in a pitcher and stir until the Equal® dissolves. Stir in the water. Taste for tartness and add a little more Equal® if desired. Add the lemon slices and serve over ice, garnish each glass with a lemon slice. Makes 4 servings.

Nutritional Analysis Per Serving:

Calories: 15	Vitamin C: . . . . .25.75 mg
Protein: . . . . .25 g	Thiamine: . . . . .02 mg
Carbohydrates: . . . . .42 g	Riboflavin: . . . . .0 mg
Fat: . . . . .0 g	Niacin. . . . . .05 mg
Phosphate: . . . . .6 mg	Calcium: . . . . .4.25 mg
Potassium: . . . . .87.25 mg	Iron: . . . . .15 mg
Zinc: . . . . .02 mg	Cholesterol: . . . . .0 mg
Vitamin A: . . . . .12.25 iu	Sodium: . . . . .75 mg

Pineappleade

1   medium fresh pineapple
2   cups water
15   packets of Equal®
¼   cup fresh mint leaves
2   tablespoons lime juice

Remove crown from pineapple. Cut off the peel. Halve pineapple; cut out core. Finely chop pineapple (about 3 cups). Place chopped pineapple in a 2 quart sauce pan. Add water. Bring to boiling; reduce heat. Cover and simmer for 15 minutes. Stir in mint. Let stand, covered, about 1½ hours or until cool. Strain; discard mint. Reserve pineapple for another use. Stir lime juice into pineapple liquid. Cover and chill. Serve over ice cubes. Add Equal® just before serving. Makes 4 servings.

Nutritional Analysis Per Serving:

Calories:. 76.75	Vitamin C: . . . . 21.25 mg
Protein: . . . . .5 g	Thiamine:. . . . . .1 mg
Carbohydrates: . . . . . 20.25 g	Riboflavin: . . . . .02 mg
Fat:. . . . . .25 g	Niacin: . . . . .25 mg
Phosphate: . . . . 10 mg	Calcium:. . . . . 20.25 mg
Potassium:. . . . . .177.5 mg	Iron: . . . . .6 mg
Zinc: . . . . :15 mg	Cholesterol: . . . . .0 mg
Vitamin A:. . . . . .82 iu	Sodium: . . . . 1.25 mg

Warming Cran-Herbal Punch

3½   cups water
2½   cups cranberry juice cocktail
8   orange herbal tea bags
6   packets of Equal®

In large saucepan, bring water and cranberry juice to a boil. Add tea bags; cover and brew 5 minutes. Remove tea bags. Stir in Equal® . Makes 6 servings.

Nutritional Analysis Per Serving:

Calories:	84	Vitamin C:	26.5 mg
Protein:	0 g	Thiamine:	.02 mg
Carbohydrates:	22.33 g	Riboflavin:	.05 mg
Fat:	0 g	Niacin:	.22 mg
Phosphate:	1 mg	Calcium:	1 mg
Potassium:	100.67 mg	Iron:	.42 mg
Zinc:	.07 mg	Cholesterol:	0 mg
Vitamin A:	0 iu	Sodium:	3.17 mg

Orange Delight

2   cups fresh orange juice
1   scoop vanilla ice cream
½   teaspoon vanilla

Place all ingredients in blender and blend at low speed until smooth. Makes two 10 ounce servings.

Nutritional Analysis Per Serving:

Calories:	179	Vitamin C:	125.5 mg
Protein:	3 g	Thiamine:	.25 mg
Carbohydrates:	34 g	Riboflavin:	.15 mg
Fat:	4 g	Niacin:	1.05 mg
Phosphate:	75.5 mg	Calcium:	71 mg
Potassium:	563.5 mg	Iron:	.55 mg
Zinc:	.4 mg	Cholesterol:	14.5 mg
Vitamin A:	634.5 iu	Sodium:	31 mg

Sparkling Fruit Punch

1½   cups boiling water
8   orange herbal tea bags
1   46 ounce can pineapple juice, chilled
2   cups pureed strawberries
2   cups chilled seltzer water

In teapot, pour boiling water over tea bags; cover and brew 5 minutes. Remove tea bags; cool. In punch bowl, combine tea, pineapple juice and strawberries. Just before serving, add seltzer water. Makes 12 servings.

Nutritional Analysis Per Serving:

Calories:........82.83	Vitamin C: ....44.67 mg
Protein: ....67 g	Thiamine: ....07 mg
Carbohydrates: .....20.08 g	Riboflavin:..........07 mg
Fat: ....25 g	Niacin:...............4 mg
Phosphate: ....16.41 mg	Calcium:..........23.92 mg
Potassium:........288.17 mg	Iron:................62 mg
Zinc:................16 mg	Cholesterol: ....0 mg
Vitamin A: ....77.33 iu	Sodium: ....1.41 mg

4

Mango Frappe

1½   cups chopped mango or banana
½   cup milk
3   packets of Equal®
1   tablespoons lime juice
¼   teaspoon vanilla
6   ice cubes

Freeze chopped fruit about 30 minutes. In a blender container combine the fruit, milk, Equal® , lime juice and vanilla. Cover; blend until smooth. With blender running, add ice cubes through lid. Blend until thick and slushy. Pour into chilled glasses. Makes 2 servings.

Nutritional Analysis Per Serving:

Calories: 127	Vitamin C: . . . . 46 mg
Protein: . . . . 3 g	Thiamine: . . . . .01 mg
Carbohydrates: . . . . 26 g	Riboflavin: . . . . .15 mg
Fat: . . . . 2.5 g	Niacin: . . . . 1.45 mg
Phosphate: . . . . 73.5 mg	Calcium: . . . . 86 mg
Potassium: . . . . 336 mg	Iron: . . . . .6 mg
Zinc: . . . . .8 mg	Cholesterol: . . . . 8.5 mg
Vitamin A: . . . . 6053.5 iu	Sodium: . . . . 38.5 mg

High Protein Milkshake

1   cup milk
1   scoop vanilla ice cream
½   teaspoon vanilla
2   tablespoons butterscotch syrup

Place all ingredients into blender. Blend at slow speed until smooth. (Note) May use chocolate or your favorite fruit syrup instead of butterscotch. Makes 1 serving.

Nutritional Analysis Per Serving:

Calories:	383	Vitamin C:	3 mg
Protein:	10 g	Thiamine:	.2 mg
Carbohydrates:	53 g	Riboflavin:	.6 mg
Fat:	15 g	Niacin:	.4 mg
Phosphate:	297 mg	Calcium:	420 mg
Potassium:	570 mg	Iron:	.8 mg
Zinc:	1.6 mg	Cholesterol:	64 mg
Vitamin A:	577 iu	Sodium:	181 mg

Strawberry Milkshake

½   cup strawberries
1   scoop vanilla ice cream
½   cup milk

Place all ingredients in blender and blend until smooth. Makes 1 serving.

Nutritional Analysis Per Serving:

Calories:	235	Vitamin C:	46 mg
Protein:	7 g	Thiamine:	1 mg
Carbohydrates:	28 g	Riboflavin:	4 mg
Fat:	12 g	Niacin:	6 mg
Phosphate:	196 mg	Calcium:	248 mg
Potassium:	435 mg	Iron:	9 mg
Zinc:	1.2 mg	Cholesterol:	46 mg
Vitamin A:	468 iu	Sodium:	118 mg

Banana Milkshake

1   ripe banana, sliced
1   cup milk
5   drops vanilla

Place all ingredients in blender and blend until smooth.
Makes 1 serving.

Nutritional Analysis Per Serving:

Calories:	250	Vitamin C:	14 mg
Protein:	9 g	Thiamine:	.2 mg
Carbohydrates:	38 g	Riboflavin:	.5 mg
Fat:	8 g	Niacin:	1.1 mg
Phosphate:	258 mg	Calcium:	301 mg
Potassium:	812 mg	Iron:	1.1 mg
Zinc:	1.2 mg	Cholesterol:	34 mg
Vitamin A:	534 iu	Sodium:	121 mg

Lime-Strawberry Slush

¼   cup fresh-squeezed lime juice
½   cup fresh strawberries
5   packets of Equal®
1   cup crushed ice

Mix together and puree in blender until slushy. Makes
1 serving.

Nutritional Analysis Per Serving:

Calories:	62	Vitamin C:	57 mg
Protein:	1 g	Thiamine:	0 mg
Carbohydrates:	17 g	Riboflavin:	.1 mg
Fat:	0 g	Niacin:	.5 mg
Phosphate:	22 mg	Calcium:	21 mg
Potassium:	186 mg	Iron:	.9 mg
Zinc:	.1 mg	Cholesterol:	0 mg
Vitamin A:	50 iu	Sodium:	1 mg

Spicy Banana Shake

1½   cups boiling water
6   toasty spice herbal tea bags
3   bananas
2   tablespoons honey
1½   cups ice cubes

In teapot, pour boiling water over tea bags; cover and brew 5 minutes. Remove tea bags; cool. In blender, combine tea, bananas and honey; process at high speed until blended. Add ice cubes, one at a time; process at high speed until blended. Makes 4 servings.

Nutritional Analysis Per Serving:

Calories: 115	Vitamin C: . . . . .9 mg
Protein: . . . . .1 g	Thiamine: . . . . .05 mg
Carbohydrates: . . . . .30 g	Riboflavin: . . . . .1 mg
Fat: . . . . .25 g	Niacin: . . . . .65 mg
Phosphate: . . . . .23.75 mg	Calcium: . . . . .7.5 mg
Potassium: . . . . .427.25 mg	Iron: . . . . .67 mg
Zinc: . . . . .25 mg	Cholesterol: . . . . .0 mg
Vitamin A: . . . . .169.5 iu	Sodium: . . . . .1.25 mg

Mocha Frost

2   cups milk
⅓   cup Suisse Mocha
1   cup coffee
1   large dip vanilla or chocolate ice cream

Place in blender and blend until smooth. Makes 2 servings.

Nutritional Analysis Per Serving:

Calories:	283.5	Vitamin C:	3 mg
Protein:	10.5 g	Thiamine:	.1 mg
Carbohydrates:	27.5 g	Riboflavin:	.55 mg
Fat:	15 g	Niacin:	.65 mg
Phosphate:	299 mg	Calcium:	381 mg
Potassium:	542.5 mg	Iron:	.45 mg
Zinc:	1.65 mg	Cholesterol:	64 mg
Vitamin A:	57.75 iu	Sodium:	178.5 mg

Fortified Milk

1   quart milk
1   cup instant non-fat dry milk

Pour liquid milk in a bowl and stir in dry milk until dissolved. Flavor improves after several hours of chilling. Makes 4 servings.

Nutritional Analysis Per Serving:

Calories:	210.25	Vitamin C:	7 mg
Protein:	14 g	Thiamine:	.17 mg
Carbohydrates:	20.5 g	Riboflavin:	.7 mg
Fat:	8.25 g	Niacin:	.4 mg
Phosphate:	395.25 mg	Calcium:	500.75 mg
Potassium:	662.25 mg	Iron:	.3 mg
Zinc:	1.67 mg	Cholesterol:	37.25 mg
Vitamin A:	711.5 iu	Sodium:	213.25 mg

Cold Bavarian Chocolate

²/₃   cup cold coffee
2   tablespoons chocolate syrup
1   scoop vanilla ice cream

Add coffee and syrup to tall glass with ice; stir. Top with ice cream. Garnish with whipped cream and chocolate curls, if you wish. Makes 1 serving.

Nutritional Analysis Per Serving:

Calories: 228	Vitamin C: . . . . .1 mg
Protein: . . . . .3 g	Thiamine: . . . . .0 mg
Carbohydrates: . . . . .40 g	Riboflavin: . . . . .2 mg
Fat: . . . . .8 g	Niacin: . . . . .7 mg
Phosphate: . . . . .107 mg	Calcium: . . . . .96 mg
Potassium: . . . . .291 mg	Iron: . . . . .8 mg
Zinc: . . . . .1.1 mg	Cholesterol: . . . . .29 mg
Vitamin A: . . . . .269 iu	Sodium: . . . . .78 mg

Tomato Refresher

2   quarts tomato juice
2   cups orange juice
¼   cup lemon juice
1   teaspoon celery salt
1   tablespoon worcestershire sauce
5   packets of Equal®
1   clove of garlic, minced

Mix all ingredients very well. Cover and chill for several hours. Makes 6 servings.

Nutritional Analysis Per Serving:

Calories: 109	Vitamin C: . . . . .89.5 mg
Protein: . . . . .3.66 g	Thiamine: . . . . .21 mg
Carbohydrates: . . . . .25.33 g	Riboflavin: . . . . .11 mg
Fat: . . . . .05 g	Niacin: . . . . .2.85 mg
Phosphate: . . . . .75.83 mg	Calcium: . . . . .34.16 mg
Potassium: . . . . . . .935.66 mg	Iron: . . . . .3.41 mg
Zinc: . . . . .25 mg	Cholesterol: . . . . .0 mg
Vitamin A: . . . . . . .2769.16 iu	Sodium: . . . . .673.33 mg

Berry Nog

2   eggs
2   tablespoons honey
1   cup apricot nectar
⅔   cup orange juice
½   cup nonfat dry milk powder
1   tablespoon lemon juice
1   cup frozen strawberries, partially thawed

In a small mixer bowl beat eggs until thick and lemon-colored. Gradually add the honey, beating constantly. Set aside. In a blender container combine the apricot nectar, orange juice, milk powder, and lemon juice; cover and blend until smooth. Cover and chill. Stir well before serving. Makes 2 servings.

Nutritional Analysis Per Serving:

Calories:.........383.5	Vitamin C:...........86 mg
Protein:.............18 g	Thiamine:...........25 mg
Carbohydrates:......67.5 g	Riboflavin:............7 mg
Fat:.................6 g	Niacin:.............1.35 mg
Phosphate:........418.5 mg	Calcium:.............439 mg
Potassium:.........1093 mg	Iron:................2.5 mg
Zinc:................2.1 mg	Cholesterol:.........2.75 mg
Vitamin A:........1643.5 iu	Sodium:.............225 mg

Apricot Tea Whirl

1½   cups boiling water
6   cinnamon apple herbal tea bags
2   12 ounce cans apricot nectar, chilled
1   cup low-fat vanilla yogurt

In teapot, pour boiling water over tea bags; cover and brew 5 minutes. Remove tea bags; cool. In blender, combine tea, apricot nectar and yogurt; process at high speed until blended. Serve over ice. Makes 6 servings.

Nutritional Analysis Per Serving:

Calories:	99	Vitamin C:	4.16 mg
Protein:	2.66 g	Thiamine:	.03 mg
Carbohydrates:	22.33 g	Riboflavin:	.13 mg
Fat:	.16 g	Niacin:	.28 mg
Phosphate:	79 mg	Calcium:	92.5 mg
Potassium:	354 mg	Iron:	.28 mg
Zinc:	.55 mg	Cholesterol:	.66 mg
Vitamin A:	1190.33 iu	Sodium:	31.33 mg

Mexican Hot Chocolate

2	ounces unsweetened chocolate
¼	cup water
2	cups milk
1	cup half and half
4	packets of Equal®
1/8	teaspoon salt
1	teaspoon ground cinnamon
1/8	teaspoon ground allspice
1/8	teaspoon ground nutmeg
1	egg
1	teaspoon vanilla
½	cup heavy cream, whipped

Melt chocolate in water in saucepan over low heat, stirring constantly. Stir in milk, half and half, salt, cinnamon, allspice and nutmeg. Bring to boiling, stirring constantly. Lower heat; simmer 10 minutes, stirring often. Beat egg in small bowl. Stir in a little of the hot chocolate mixture; return to saucepan, stirring. Add vanilla. Cook 3 minutes, stirring constantly. Pour into cups or mugs, add one packet of Equal® to each cup, stir, and top with whipped cream. Makes 4 servings.

Nutritional Analysis Per Serving:

Calories:	348.5	Vitamin C:	2.25 mg
Protein:	9.25 g	Thiamine:	.1 mg
Carbohydrates:	14.25 g	Riboflavin:	.37 mg
Fat:	30.75 g	Niacin:	.04 mg
Phosphate:	267.5 mg	Calcium:	245.25 mg
Potassium:	417.5 mg	Iron:	1.35 mg
Zinc:	1.12 mg	Cholesterol:	142 mg
Vitamin A:	922.5 iu	Sodium:	112 mg

Orange Sunrise

2   eggs
¼   cup frozen concentrated orange juice
2   tablespoons honey
2   cups cold milk
1   8 ounce container orange yogurt

Place eggs, orange juice and honey in blender container and blend until smooth, about 1 minute. Add milk and yogurt. Blend until smooth and frothy. Serve immediately in tall, chilled glasses. Makes 3 servings.

Nutritional Analysis Per Serving:

Calories: 265	Vitamin C: . . . . 11 mg
Protein: . . . . 12.67 g	Thiamine: . . . . 13 mg
Carbohydrates: . . . . . 37.67 g	Riboflavin: . . . . 53 mg
Fat: . . . . 7.33 g	Niacin: . . . . 37 mg
Phosphate: . . . . 310.67 mg	Calcium: . . . . 342.62 mg
Potassium: . . . . 498.33 mg	Iron: . . . . 1.03 mg
Zinc: . . . . 1.70 mg	Cholesterol: . . . . 180.67 mg
Vitamin A: . . . . 570 iu	Sodium: . . . . 171.33 mg

Gazpacho de Madrid

4	tomatoes, peeled and chopped
⅓	green bell pepper
⅓	cucumber, peeled
¼	onion, chopped
2	garlic cloves
3	tablespoons red-wine vinegar
2	tablespoons olive oil
3	cups french bread cubes, crusts removed, soaked in water

In a blender or food processor puree the tomatoes, green pepper, cucumber, onion and garlic. Blend in the vinegar and oil and the bread crumbs in batches. Pour mixture into bowl and thin to desired consistency with ice water and chill in covered bowl overnight. Serve in chilled bowls. Makes 4 servings.

Nutritional Analysis Per Serving:

Calories:	211	Vitamin C:	45.5 mg
Protein:	5.25 g	Thiamine:	.25 mg
Carbohydrates:	29.75 g	Riboflavin:	.15 mg
Fat:	8.5 g	Niacin:	2.2 mg
Phosphate:	76.5 mg	Calcium:	49.75 mg
Potassium:	385.75 mg	Iron:	1.7 mg
Zinc:	.55 mg	Cholesterol:	1 mg
Vitamin A:	1069 iu	Sodium:	1495 mg

Carrot and Orange Soup

2	tablespoons butter
1	tablespoon cooking oil
1	pound carrots, sliced
2	medium onions, chopped
2	tablespoons flour
1½	pints chicken stock
½	orange, grated rind and juice
½	lemon, juice
	salt and pepper

Heat the butter and oil in a saucepan, add carrot and onion and fry until softened. Sprinkle in flour and cook for 1 minute, stirring. Add the orange rind and juice, lemon juice, salt and pepper to taste. Cover and simmer for 30 minutes. Cool slightly, then blend in a blender until smooth. Reheat before serving. Makes 4 servings.

Nutritional Analysis Per Serving:

Calories:	206.25	Vitamin C:	40.25 mg
Protein:	4 g	Thiamine:	.18 mg
Carbohydrates:	28.5 g	Riboflavin:	.13 mg
Fat:	9.75 g	Niacin:	1.5 mg
Phosphate:	91 mg	Calcium:	91 mg
Potassium:	757.75 mg	Iron:	1.73 mg
Zinc:	.98 mg	Cholesterol:	18 mg
Vitamin A:	20076 iu	Sodium:	1046.5 mg

Chestnut Soup

1   stick unsalted butter
1   large onion, coarsely chopped
2   medium carrots, coarsley chopped
¼   cup all-purpose flour
2   quarts chicken stock or canned broth
1   pound peeled, cooked chestnuts
¼   teaspoon white pepper
2   cups heavy cream (optional)

In a large saucepan, melt the butter over moderate heat. Add the onion and carrots and saute, stirring occasionally, until the onion is softened and translucent, about 5 minutes.

Sprinkle on the flour and stir to coat the vegetables. Cook stirring, for 2 minutes.

Whisk in the chicken stock, 1 cup at a time. Add the chestnuts and season with the pepper. Simmer, uncovered until the soup is slightly thickened, about 30 minutes.

Puree the soup in batches in blender or food processor until completely smooth. Add cream, if desired, and reheat. Serve hot. Makes 8 servings.

Nutritional Analysis Per Serving:

Calories:	360.88	Vitamin C:	3.38 mg
Protein:	3.5 g	Thiamine:	.08 mg
Carbohydrates:	12.25 g	Riboflavin:	.13 mg
Fat:	34 g	Niacin:	.41 mg
Phosphate:	65.13 mg	Calcium:	57.88 mg
Potassium:	187 mg	Iron:	.53 mg
Zinc:	.31 mg	Cholesterol:	116.63 mg
Vitamin A:	3297.5iu	Sodium:	1259.01 mg

Vegetable Soup

4	teaspoons butter
2	strips bacon, chopped
2	onions, chopped
2	leeks, chopped
1	parsnip, chopped
2	carrots, chopped
1	potato, chopped
1½	pints beef stock
8	ounce can tomatoes
2	bay leaves
¼	teaspoon thyme
1	tablespoon parsley, chopped
	salt and pepper

Melt butter in large saucepan, add bacon and fry slowly. Add the vegetables and cook until they are soft, adding more butter if necessary. Pour in the stock and add the tomatoes with juice, herbs, salt and pepper to taste. Bring to a boil and cook for 40 minutes. Cool and remove bay leaves. Place in blender until smooth. Reheat before serving. Makes 2 servings.

Nutritional Analysis Per Serving:

Calories:	*432*	*Vitamin C:*	*59.5 mg*
Protein:	*9.5 g*	*Thiamine:*	*.3 mg*
Carbohydrates:	*39.5 g*	*Riboflavin:*	*.2 mg*
Fat:	*28 g*	*Niacin:*	*2.9 mg*
Phosphate:	*175.5 mg*	*Calcium:*	*137 mg*
Potassium:	*1175 mg*	*Iron:*	*2.9 mg*
Zinc:	*1.4 mg*	*Cholesterol:*	*74 mg*
Vitamin A:	*10082.5 iu*	*Sodium:*	*2319.5 mg*

Autumn Bisque Soup

1	pound butternut squash, pared, halved, seeded and cubed
2	tart apples, pared, cored, cubed
1	medium-sized onion, chopped (½ cup)
2	slices white bread, trimmed and cubed
4	cups chicken broth
¼	teaspoon pepper
¼	teaspoon ground rosemary
¼	teaspoon marjoram
2	egg yolks, slightly beaten
¼	cup heavy cream

Combine the squash, apples, onion, bread, chicken broth, pepper, rosemary and marjoram in large saucepan. Bring to boiling. Lower heat; simmer, uncovered, 35 minutes or until squash and apples are tender. Remove from heat and cool to luke warm.

Working in batches, spoon the soup into the container of an electric blender or food processor. Cover; whirl until pureed. Return the soup to the saucepan. Reheat the soup gently over very low heat.

Mix together the egg yolks and the cream in a small bowl. Beat in a little of the hot soup; return yolk mixture to the saucepan, stirring. Heat gently to serve; do not boil or the eggs will curdle. Garnish with a fresh rosemary sprig if you wish. Makes 6 servings.

Nutritional Analysis Per Serving:

Calories:	142.5	Vitamin C:	9.83 mg
Protein:	3.67 g	Thiamine:	.1 mg
Carbohydrates:	20 g	Riboflavin:	.15 mg
Fat:	6.17 g	Niacin:	.68 mg
Phosphate:	76.33 mg	Calcium:	48.16 mg
Potassium:	307.67 mg	Iron:	1.1 mg
Zinc:	.57 mg	Cholesterol:	96.5 mg
Vitamin A:	3144.33 iu	Sodium:	948 mg

Green Bean Soup

½   cup finely chopped onion
1   tablespoon chopped parsley
2   tablespoons butter
5   cups cooked and chopped green beans
1   cup sour cream
½   cup grated American cheese
½   cup bread crumbs
2   tablespoons melted butter
2   tablespoons flour
½   tablespoon pepper

Cook first three ingredients until tender, but not brown. Then stir in and cook last three ingredients. Add sour cream and mix well. Add green beans, heat and stir. Pour all into greased baking dish and top with grated cheese. Mix bread crumbs and melted butter, sprinkle on top. Heat at 325 degrees in oven for 25 minutes or until soft. Makes 8 servings.

Nutritional Analysis Per Serving:

Calories:	183.75	Vitamin C:	12.13 mg
Protein:	4.88 g	Thiamine:	11 mg
Carbohydrates:	12.5 g	Riboflavin:	18 mg
Fat:	13.38 g	Niacin:	88 mg
Phosphate:	121.25 mg	Calcium:	132.5 mg
Potassium:	203.63 mg	Iron:	93 mg
Zinc:	61 mg	Cholesterol:	32.75 mg
Vitamin A:	992.13 iu	Sodium:	365.5 mg

French Onion Soup

4   large onions, thinly sliced and chopped
¼   cup butter
3   10½ ounce cans condensed beef broth
1   teaspoon worcestershire sauce
        dash of pepper

Cook onions in butter until lightly browned, about 20 minutes. Add broth and worcestershire. Bring to boiling. Season with pepper. Sprinkle cheese on top and place under broiler to melt cheese. Makes 6 servings.

Nutritional Analysis Per Serving:

Calories:..........90.83		Vitamin C: ....4.67 mg
Protein: ....1.5 g		Thiamine:...........02 mg
Carbohydrates: ......4.67 g		Riboflavin: ....02 mg
Fat:...............7.67 g		Niacin: ....13 mg
Phosphate: ....22.17 mg		Calcium:...........20.33 mg
Potassium:.........85.67 mg		Iron: ....33 mg
Zinc: ....23 mg		Cholesterol:........22.83 mg
Vitamin A: ....314.83 iu		Sodium: ....922.17 mg

Tomato Ham Surprise

1   can of tomato soup
1   5 ounce can of potted ham
1   cup milk

Mix all ingredients together and heat over moderate heat. Stir to prevent sticking. Serve hot and refrigerate any unused portion. Makes 2 servings.

Nutritional Analysis Per Serving:

Calories:	480	Vitamin C:	19 mg
Protein:	21.5 g	Thiamine:	.4 mg
Carbohydrates:	29.5 g	Riboflavin:	.5 mg
Fat:	31 g	Niacin:	4.25 mg
Phosphate:	290.5 mg	Calcium:	217 mg
Potassium:	721.5 mg	Iron:	2.9 mg
Zinc:	4 mg	Cholesterol:	101.5 mg
Vitamin A:	1500 iu	Sodium:	2429 mg

Pea Soup Supreme

1   can of green pea soup
1   6 ounce can of potted meat
½   cup milk
     dash pepper

Mix all ingredients in saucepan and bring to a boil. Serve hot. Makes 2 servings.

Nutritional Analysis Per Serving:

Calories:	530	Vitamin C:	12.5 mg
Protein:	26.5 g	Thiamine:	.4 mg
Carbohydrates:	37.5 g	Riboflavin:	.55 mg
Fat:	30.5 g	Niacin:	4.25 mg
Phosphate:	390.5 mg	Calcium:	254.5 mg
Potassium:	677.5 mg	Iron:	3.25 mg
Zinc:	5.45 mg	Cholesterol:	101.5 mg
Vitamin A:	656 iu	Sodium:	2338.5 mg

Quick Mushroom Soup

4   tablespoons butter
3½   tablespoons flour
1   pint chicken stock
½   pint milk
½   cup mushrooms, finely chopped
1   clove garlic, crushed
1   tablespoon lemon juice
1   tablespoon parsley, finely chopped
4   ounces cream
       salt and pepper
       paprika to garnish

Melt butter in saucepan and stir in flour. Cook, stirring for 1 minute. Add stock and milk, bring to a boil, stirring constantly. Add mushrooms, garlic, salt and pepper to taste and lemon juice. Simmer for 5 minutes then stir in parsley and cream. Serve hot and garnish with paprika. Makes 2 servings.

Nutritional Analysis Per Serving:

Calories:. 546.5		Vitamin C:. . . . . .9 mg	
Protein: . . . . .8.5 g		Thiamine:. . . . . .2 mg	
Carbohydrates:. . . . . . . .20 g		Riboflavin: . . . . .4 mg	
Fat:. . . . . .49.5 g		Niacin: . . . . .1.65 mg	
Phosphate: . . . . .192 mg		Calcium· . . . . .199 mg	
Potassium: . . . . .354 mg		Iron: . . . . .85 mg	
Zinc: . . . . .95 mg		Cholesterol: . . . . .164 mg	
Vitamin A:. . . . . .2064 iu		Sodium: . . . . .1518 mg	

Mushroom-Clam Velorte

2   tablespoons unsalted butter
¼   cup all-purpose flour
2   cups fresh clam liquor or 2 bottles clam juice
10   ounces of fresh mushrooms
1   cup heavy cream
½   teaspoon ground pepper
      salt

Mince mushrooms in food processor or blender and set aside. In a medium saucepan, cook the butter and flour together over moderate heat, stirring constantly, until brown, 6 to 10 minutes.

Add the clam liquor, mushrooms and ⅔ cup of water and stir briskly to combine. Bring to a boil, reduce heat and simmer, stirring occasionally, for 15 minutes to blend.

Whisk in the cream and pepper and simmer for 5 minutes. Season with salt to taste. Makes 4 servings.

Nutritional Analysis Per Serving:

Calories:.........313.25	Vitamin C: ....1.25 mg
Protein: ....5.5 g	Thiamine:........... .08 mg
Carbohydrates:........11 g	Riboflavin: .... .18 mg
Fat: ....28.25 g	Niacin: ....1.15 mg
Phosphate: ....65.75 mg	Calcium:...........42.75 mg
Potassium:.........126.5 mg	Iron: .... .38 mg
Zinc: .... .43 mg	Cholesterol:.......108.25 mg
Vitamin A: ....1096 iu	Sodium: ....506.25 mg

Leek and Potato Soup

4   tablespoons butter
1   tablespoon oil
6   leeks, sliced
4   potatoes, sliced
2   pints chicken stock
6   ounces cream
      salt and pepper
      pinch of grated nutmeg

In large saucepan heat butter and oil. Add leeks and fry until softened. Add potatoes, stock, salt and pepper to taste and nutmeg. Cover and cook for 30 minutes. Cool and place in blender until smooth. Return to saucepan, add cream and heat being careful not to boil. Makes 6 servings.

Nutritional Analysis Per Serving:

Calories:..........805.5		Vitamin C:............59 mg	
Protein:..............11 g		Thiamine:...........35 mg	
Carbohydrates:.......52 g		Riboflavin:..........25 mg	
Fat:.................64 g		Niacin:..............3.7 mg	
Phosphate:..........219 mg		Calcium:...........126.5 mg	
Potassium:.........1156 mg		Iron:...............2.35 mg	
Zinc:................1.3 mg		Cholesterol:.........192 mg	
Vitamin A:..........2214 iu		Sodium:..........2675.5 mg	

Potato and Turnip Soup

3   large potatoes, peeled and cubed
2   large turnips, peeled and cubed
1   large onion, peeled and cubed
1   teaspoon butter
6   ounces of American cheese

Combine all ingredients except cheese in a saucepan and cover with water. Bring to a boil and cook until soft. Drain off water and whip with a mixer. In another pan melt cheese and add to mixture blending in well. Milk may be added to thin soup. Makes 4 servings.

Nutritional Analysis Per Serving:

Calories: 127.25	Vitamin C: . . . . 19.25 mg
Protein: . . . . 6 g	Thiamine: . . . . .05 mg
Carbohydrates: . . . . . . 9.25 g	Riboflavin: . . . . .13 mg
Fat: . . . . 7.75 g	Niacin: . . . . .68 mg
Phosphate: . . . . 190.5 mg	Calcium: . . . . 155 mg
Potassium: . . . . 251.25 mg	Iron: . . . . .53 mg
Zinc: . . . . .9 mg	Cholesterol: . . . . 22.25 mg
Vitamin A: . . . . 300 iu	Sodium: . . . . 428 mg

Catfish Soup

1   2 pound catfish, boned and cut up
2   quarts of water
1   onion, finely chopped
1   stalk of celery, finely chopped
1   cup milk
2   tablespoons butter
     salt and pepper to taste

Combine all ingredients in a large pot and bring to a boil. Reduce heat and simmer until fish flakes easily. Serves 8.

Nutritional Analysis Per Serving (continued on page 27)

CATFISH SOUP *(continued from page 26)*

Nutritional Analysis Per Serving:

Calories: 159	Vitamin C: . . . . 1.38 mg
Protein: . . . . 20.75 g	Thiamine: . . . . 0.06 mg
Carbohydrates: . . . . . . 2.38 g	Riboflavin: . . . . 0.09 mg
Fat: . . . . 6.88 g	Niacin: . . . . 1.95 mg
Phosphate: . . . . 304.5 mg	Calcium: . . . . 67.5 mg
Potassium: . . . . 435.5 mg	Iron: . . . . 0.54 mg
Zinc: . . . . 1.28 mg	Cholesterol: . . . . 71.25 mg
Vitamin A: . . . . 290.5 iu	Sodium: . . . . 114.25 mg

Cheese Chowder

¼ cup finely chopped onion

2 tablespoons butter

¼ cup all-purpose flour

2 cups milk

1 13¾ ounce can chicken broth

¼ cup finely diced carrot

¼ cup finely diced celery

  dash of salt and paprika

½ cup sharp process American cheese

Cook onion in butter until tender. Blend in flour; add remaining ingredients except cheese. Cook and stir until thick and bubbly. Reduce heat; add cheese; stir to melt. Simmer 15 minutes. Makes 4 servings.

Nutritional Analysis Per Serving:

Calories: 216.75	Vitamin C: . . . . 3.75 mg
Protein: . . . . 8.75 g	Thiamine: . . . . .13 mg
Carbohydrates: . . . . 14 g	Riboflavin: . . . . .3 mg
Fat: . . . . 14.25 g	Niacin: . . . . .65 mg
Phosphate: . . . . 236.75 mg	Calcium: . . . . 245.25 mg
Potassium: . . . . 289.5 mg	Iron: . . . . .55 mg
Zinc: . . . . 1 mg	Cholesterol: . . . . 47 mg
Vitamin A: . . . . 1550.25 iu	Sodium: . . . . 786 mg

Cheddar Asparagus Soup

¾   stick butter
¾   cup finely chopped onion
¾   cup finely chopped celery
½   cup all purpose flour
6   cups chicken stock, heated to simmer
½   teaspoon crumbled bay leaf
¼   cup sherry
     dash - hot pepper sauce
     dash - worcestershire sauce
     pinch - dry mustard
     ground pepper
1   pound small fresh asparagus, trimmed and cut into small pieces
10   ounces mild cheddar cheese, shredded

Melt butter in large skillet over medium heat. Add onion and celery and cook, stirring frequently, until tender but not brown, about 8 minutes. Reduce heat to low, add flour and cook, stirring frequently, until frothy, 5 to 10 minutes. Blend in chicken stock and bay leaf. Increase heat to high and bring to boil. Reduce heat to medium-low. Add sherry, hot pepper sauce, worcestershire, dry mustard and ground pepper and simmer 20 minutes.

Add asparagus and continue cooking until tender, about 10 minutes. Place soup in blender or food processor and blend until smooth.

Return soup to large skillet, add cheese and stir until cheese melts. Ladle soup into heated bowls and serve immediately. Makes 6 servings.

Nutritional Analysis Per Serving (continued on page 29)

Nutritional Analysis Per Serving:

Calories:............362.33	Vitamin C: ....10.33 mg
Protein: ....15.17 g	Thiamine:........... .13 mg
Carbohydrates: .....12.83 g	Riboflavin: .... .28 mg
Fat:...............27.17 g	Niacin:................1 mg
Phosphate: ....282.83 mg	Calcium:..........361.33 mg
Potassium:.......221.67 mg	Iron: ....1.17 mg
Zinc: ....1.92 mg	Cholesterol:........83.33 mg
Vitamin A: ....1232.17 iu	Sodium: ....1631.33 mg

Guacamole Soup

1	13¾ ounce can chicken broth
2	medium avocados, seeded, peeled, and cut into chunks
1	4 ounce can green chili pepers, rinsed and seeded
1	slice onion
2	tablespoons lemon juice
1	cup light cream or milk
1	large tomato, peeled, seeded and chopped

In a blender or food processor combine all ingredients and blend until smooth. Cover, chill well and serve. Makes 4 servings.

Nutritional Analysis Per Serving:

Calories: 325	Vitamin C:............33 mg
Protein:..............5 g	Thiamine:........... .18 mg
Carbohydrates: .....11.75 g	Riboflavin: .... .33 mg
Fat: ....31 g	Niacin: ....2.15 mg
Phosphate: ....106.5 mg	Calcium:...........76.25 mg
Potassium: ....897 mg	Iron: .... .9 mg
Zinc: ....7 mg	Cholesterol:........41.5 mg
Vitamin A: ....1072.5 iu	Sodium: . ...680.25 mg

Acorn Squash Soup

2	pounds acorn squash, halved and seeded
2	tablespoons (¼ stick) butter
2	large leeks, whites only, chopped
5	cups chicken stock
1	tablespoon tomato paste
1	large thyme sprig or ½ teaspoon dried and crumbled
¼	teaspoon salt
·	ground white pepper
½	cup cream

Preheat oven to 350 degrees. Arrange squash cut side down in roasting pan. Add ½ inch water. Bake until squash begins to soften, about 30 minutes.

Melt butter in large saucepan over medium heat. Add leeks, cover and cook until translucent, stirring occasionally, about 5 minutes. Scoop out squash pulp and add to leeks. Blend in stock, tomato paste, thyme, salt and pepper. Simmer until squash is very soft, about 20 minutes. Cool slightly. Discard fresh thyme (if using).

Puree soup in blender until smooth. Rewarm soup in saucepan over medium-low heat. Stir in cream and heat through; do not boil. Serve hot. Makes 6 servings.

Nutritional Analysis Per Serving:

Calories:	405.5	Vitamin C:	20.17 mg
Protein:	5.17 g	Thiamine:	.1 mg
Carbohydrates:	24.5 g	Riboflavin:	.27 mg
Fat:	34.17 g	Niacin:	1 mg
Phosphate:	121.17 mg	Calcium:	97 mg
Potassium:	728.83 mg	Iron:	1.22 mg
Zinc:	.63 mg	Cholesterol:	122.83 mg
Vitamin A:	7062.5 iu	Sodium:	1167.67 mg

Sweet Pepper Puree

5   medium-sized red, yellow or green bell peppers, seeded and cut into one inch chunks

6   cups cold chicken broth

1   medium-sized red onion, cut into one inch chunks

1   medium boiling potato, peeled and cut into one inch chunks

8   bay leaves

¼   teaspoon dried thyme, crumbled

1   whole clove

6   scant teaspoons olive oil
       salt and ground pepper

Soak peppers in cold water 30 minutes. Drain peppers and combine with broth, onion and potato in heavy medium saucepan over medium heat. Cover and simmer until vegetables are tender, about 45 minutes.

Puree soup through fine disc of food mill or in food processor. Return to saucepan. Wrap 2 bay leaves, thyme and clove in cheesecloth and add to soup. Season with salt and pepper. Bring to simmer and cook until thick, stirring occasionally, about 25 minutes.

Soak remaining bay leaves in luke-warm water to cover 5 minutes and drain. Discard cheesecloth package. Ladle soup into bowls. Top each with bay leaf and drizzle with olive oil in "C" pattern. Serve hot or cold. Makes 8 servings.

Nutritional Analysis Per Serving:

Calories:...........72.88	Vitamin C:...........135 mg
Protein: ....2.5 g	Thiamine:............ .1 mg
Carbohydrates: ....8.5 g	Riboflavin: .... .09 mg
Fat:................3.88 g	Niacin: .... .74 mg
Phosphate: ....33.38 mg	Calcium: ....13 mg
Potassium:........286.75 mg	Iron: ... . .88 mg
Zinc: .... .15 mg	Cholesterol:.........2.75 mg
Vitamin A: ....434.75 iu	Sodium: ....914.63 mg

Broccoli Soup

1	10 ounce package frozen chopped broccoli
1½	cups milk
1	cup light cream
1	teaspoon instant minced onion
2	beef bouillon cubes
¼	teaspoon salt
	dash pepper
	dash ground nutmeg
	dairy sour cream

Partially thaw broccoli; break into small chunks. Place in blender container with ½ cup of milk. Blend until smooth, 40 to 60 seconds. Add all other ingredients and blend another 30 to 40 seconds. Chill thoroughly. Serve topped with dollops of dairy sour cream. Makes 4 servings.

Nutritional Analysis Per Serving:

Calories:	301.75	Vitamin C:	34.75 mg
Protein:	7.25 g	Thiamine:	.1 mg
Carbohydrates:	10.25 g	Riboflavin:	.33 mg
Fat:	26.75 g	Niacin:	.4 mg
Phosphate:	175.75 mg	Calcium:	211.25 mg
Potassium:	362 mg	Iron:	.53 mg
Zinc:	.85 mg	Cholesterol:	91.75 mg
Vitamin A:	2485.25 iu	Sodium:	832.25 mg

Two Melon Soup

1   small very ripe cantaloupe, peeled, seeded, and chopped
2   tablespoons fresh lemon juice, or to taste
½   very ripe honeydew melon, peeled, seeded and chopped
3   tablespoons fresh lime juice or to taste
1½   teaspoons minced fresh mint, or to taste
    sour cream for garnish

In a food processor or blender puree the cantaloupe with lemon juice in batches until it is very smooth, chill; covered for at least 3 hours or overnight. In a food processor or blender puree the honeydew with the lime juice and the minced mint in batches until it is very smooth, and chill, covered, for at least 3 hours or overnight. Pour at the same time, using 2 cups, equal amounts of both soups into chilled bowls and garnish each serving with sour cream. Makes 6 servings.

Nutritional Analysis Per Serving:

Calories:............97.5	Vitamin C: ....56.83 mg
Protein: ....2 g	Thiamine............08 mg
Carbohydrates: .....16.17 g	Riboflavin: ....08 mg
Fat:................3.83 g	Niacin: ....1.17 mg
Phosphate: ....45.33 mg	Calcium:...........46.17 mg
Potassium:........516.33 mg	Iron: ....8 mg
Zinc: ....3 mg	Cholesterol: ....7 mg
Vitamin A: ....3250.67 iu	Sodium: ....31.33 mg

Chilled Spanish Tomato Soup

1   pound tomatoes, skinned and chopped
1   onion, chopped
1   green pepper, chopped
1   clove garlic, crushed
1   tablespoon wine vinegar
2   tablespoons olive oil
2   tablespoons lemon juice
1   slice white bread, crust removed
½   pint chicken stock
    salt and pepper

Place all ingredients in blender and blend until smooth. Chill overnight in covered bowl before serving. Makes 2 servings.

Nutritional Analysis Per Serving:

Calories:...........246.5		Vitamin C:...........153 mg	
Protein: ....5.5 g		Thiamine:........... .25 mg	
Carbohydrates:........25 g		Riboflavin: .... .2 mg	
Fat: ....15 g		Niacin: ....2.6 mg	
Phosphate: ....91.5 mg		Calcium:...........106.5 mg	
Potassium: ....788 mg		Iron: ....2.35 mg	
Zinc: .... .75 mg		Cholesterol: .... .2 mg	
Vitamin A: ....2522.5 iu		Sodium:.............990 mg	

Chicken Mushroom Soup

1   can condensed cream of mushroom soup
1   can condensed cream of chicken soup
1   cup water
      dash pepper

Mix in saucepan and bring to a boil. Serve hot. Makes 2 servings.

Nutritional Analysis Per Serving:

Calories: 285	Vitamin C: . . . . 0 mg
Protein: . . . . 6.5 g	Thiamine: . . . . .05 mg
Carbohydrates: . . . . . . 22.5 g	Riboflavin: . . . . .2 mg
Fat: . . . . 19 g	Niacin: . . . . 1.5 mg
Phosphate: . . . . 105 mg	Calcium: . . . . .81 mg
Potassium: . . . . 222 mg	Iron: . . . . .1.2 mg
Zinc: . . . . 1.5 mg	Cholesterol: . . . . .24 mg
Vitamin A: . . . . .600 iu	Sodium: . . . . .2406 mg

Chicken Curry Soup

1   can of cream of chicken soup
1¼ cups milk
½   teaspoon curry powder

Mix well and chill for 3 to 4 hours. Makes 2 servings.

Nutritional Analysis Per Serving:

Calories: 357.5	Vitamin C: . . . . 5 mg
Protein: . . . . 14.5 g	Thiamine: . . . . .1 mg
Carbohydrates: . . . . 29 g	Riboflavin: . . . . .55 mg
Fat: . . . . 20.5 g	Niacin: . . . . .1.45 mg
Phosphate: . . . . .303.5 mg	Calcium: . . . . .343 mg
Potassium: . . . . 519 mg	Iron: . . . . .1 mg
Zinc: . . . . 1.3 mg	Cholesterol: . . . . .53.5 mg
Vitamin A: . . . . 1225 iu	Sodium: . . . . .2107 mg

Chicken Velvet Soup

6   tablespoons butter
1/3   cup all-purpose flour
1/2   cup milk
1/2   cup light cream
3   cups chicken broth
1   cup finely chopped cooked chicken

Melt butter in saucepan. Blend in flour; add milk, cream, and broth. Cook and stir until mixture thickens and comes to a boil; reduce heat. Stir in chicken and dash pepper. Heat again just to boiling; serve immediately. Garnish with snipped parsley and pimento if desired. Makes 4 servings.

Nutritional Analysis Per Serving:

Calories: 365.5	Vitamin C: . . . . .5 mg
Protein: . . . . 15.75 g	Thiamine: . . . . .1 mg
Carbohydrates: . . . . . . 10.5 g	Riboflavin: . . . . 18 mg
Fat: . . . . 29.25 g	Niacin: . . . . 3.9 mg
Phosphate: . . . . . . 127.25 mg	Calcium: . . . . 69.25 mg
Potassium: . . . . 170.25 mg	Iron: . . . . .75 mg
Zinc: . . . . .78 mg	Cholesterol: . . . . . . 118.75 mg
Vitamin A: . . . . 1030 iu	Sodium: . . . . 1126.25 mg

Cold Peach Soup

5   large ripe peaches peeled and quartered
6   packets of Equal®
1   cup sour cream
1/4   cup fresh lemon juice
2   tablespoons thawed orange juice concentrate

Puree 5 peaches with Equal® in food processor or blender. Mix in sour cream. Add lemon juice, and orange concentrate and blend until smooth. Transfer to bowl. Cover and refrigerate until well chilled. Ladle soup into bowls and serve. Makes 4 servings.

Nutritional Analysis Per Serving *(continued on page 37)*

COLD PEACH SOUP *(continued from page 36)*

Nutritional Analysis Per Serving:

Calories:	200	Vitamin C:	23 mg
Protein:	3 g	Thiamine:	.08 mg
Carbohydrates:	27.25 g	Riboflavin:	.20 mg
Fat:	10.25 g	Niacin:	2.38 mg
Phosphate:	86.25 mg	Calcium:	77.5 mg
Potassium:	557.75 mg	Iron:	1.23 mg
Zinc:	.60 mg	Cholesterol:	21 mg
Vitamin A:	3457.75 iu	Sodium:	27.75 mg

Chilled Asparagus Soup

1	10 ounce package frozen cut asparagus
2	cups milk
1	teaspoon instant minced onion
1	teaspoon salt
	dash pepper
½	cup light cream
½	cup dairy sour cream

Cook asparagus according to package directions; drain well. Combine asparagus with one cup of the milk, the onions, salt, and pepper in a blender container, blend until smooth, about 10 seconds. Add remaining milk; blend 5 seconds longer. Add light cream; blend 5 seconds. Chill 3 to 4 hours. Top servings with dollops of sour cream. Makes 4 servings.

Nutritional Analysis Per Serving:

Calories:	223	Vitamin C:	10.5 mg
Protein:	6.75 g	Thiamine:	.13 mg
Carbohydrates:	9.25 g	Riboflavin:	.33 mg
Fat:	18.5 g	Niacin:	.53 mg
Phosphate:	178.25 mg	Calcium:	206.75 mg
Potassium:	336.75 mg	Iron:	.6 mg
Zinc:	.98 mg	Cholesterol:	61 mg
Vitamin A:	1001.25 iu	Sodium:	644.75 mg

Creamy Cold Avocado Soup

3	tablespoons unsalted butter
3	tablespoons all-purpose flour
3	cups canned chicken broth
3	avocados peeled and pitted
1	cup sour cream
1½	tablespoons fresh lemon juice
½	teaspoon white pepper
2	scallions, minced
1	small fresh hot red pepper, minced,
OR	
¼	teaspoon cayenne pepper
1	tablespoon olive oil

In a heavy medium saucepan, melt the butter over low heat. Whisk in the flour until smooth and cook, stirring, for 2 minutes without coloring to make a roux. Add the chicken broth and whisk until smooth. Bring to a boil, stirring; reduce heat to low and simmer, uncovered, for 5 minutes. Pour into a shallow container and place in the freezer until cool, 20 to 30 minutes.

Cut avocados into large chunks and puree in a blender or food processor. Add the sour cream and puree until blended.

Pour in half of the chicken broth and puree until well blended. Pour into a large bowl. Whisk in the remaining broth, lemon juice, white pepper and ½ cup of cold water. Refrigerate, covered, until chilled, about 3 hours.

In a small bowl, combine the scallions, hot red pepper, and olive oil. To serve, divide the soup among 6 bowls and drop about one-half tablespoon of the scallion-pepper oil into the center of each. Makes 6 servings.

Nutritional Analysis Per Serving (continued on page 39)

CREAMY COLD AVOCADO SOUP *(continued from page 38)*

Nutritional Analysis Per Serving:

Calories:.........352.67	Vitamin C: ....18.33 mg
Protein: ....4.5 g	Thiamine:...........17 mg
Carbohydrates: .....11.83 g	Riboflavin: ....3 mg
Fat:...............34.17 g	Niacin: ....2.07 mg
Phosphate: ....81 mg	Calcium:...........51.83 mg
Potassium:.........749.5 mg	Iron: ....87 mg
Zinc: ....6 mg	Cholesterol:........31.17 mg
Vitamin A: ....796.67 iu	Sodium: ....622.33 mg

Cauliflower Soup

1	medium head cauliflower, finely chopped
¼	cup butter
⅔	cup onion, finely chopped
2	tablespoons flour
2	cans of chicken broth
2	cups of light cream
½	tablespoon worcestershire sauce
	parsley for garnish

Cook cauliflower in boiling water until tender. Drain and reserve liquid. Melt butter and add the onion, cooking until onion is soft. Blend in flour, add broth and cook until the mixture comes to a boil, stirring constantly. Stir in 1 cup of liquid drained from cauliflower, cream, worcestershire sauce, and cauliflower. When this mixture comes to a boil, reduce heat and simmer for 2 minutes. Garnish with parsley. Makes 2 servings.

Nutritional Analysis Per Serving:

Calories: 775	Vitamin C: ....58.5 mg
Protein: ....15.5 g	Thiamine: ....25 mg
Carbohydrates: ......26.5 g	Riboflavin:..........55 mg
Fat:................69.5 g	Niacin: ....2.55 mg
Phosphate: ....301.5 mg	Calcium:...........296.5 mg
Potassium: ....733 mg	Iron: ....1.9 mg
Zinc: ....1.6 mg	Cholesterol:........244.5 mg
Vitamin A: ....2691 iu	Sodium:............2616 mg

Pumpkin Soup

1	large onion, sliced
¼	cup butter
½	teaspoon curry powder
2	cups canned pumpkin
1½	teaspoons salt
2	cups heavy cream
2½	cups chicken stock

Melt butter in skillet, add the onion and saute until soft. Sprinkle with curry powder and saute an additional few minutes. Add curried onions, pumpkin and salt to food processor or blender. Process until well mixed, then pour in heavy cream, while continuing to process. Transfer pumpkin puree to a large saucepan and heat slowly with chicken stock. Serve steaming hot. Makes 4 servings.

Nutritional Analysis Per Serving:

Calories:	*577*	*Vitamin C:*	*9 mg*
Protein:	*6.25 g*	*Thiamine:*	*2.23 mg*
Carbohydrates:	*16 g*	*Riboflavin:*	*.13 mg*
Fat:	*56.25 g*	*Niacin:*	*.05 mg*
Phosphate:	*163 mg*	*Calcium:*	*.18 mg*
Potassium:	*497.25 mg*	*Iron:*	*.1 mg*
Zinc:	*.75 mg*	*Cholesterol:*	*.15 mg*
Vitamin A:	*10079.75 iu*	*Sodium:*	*.08 mg*

Salmon Tetrazzini

1   pound can salmon
2   tablespoons butter, melted
2   tablespoons flour
2   cups cooked spaghetti, finely chopped
4   ounces mushrooms, drained and finely chopped
2   tablespoons parmesan cheese
2   tablespoons dry bread crumbs
     dash each of pepper and nutmeg
     milk

Drain salmon, reserving liquid. Add enough milk to reserved liquid to measure 2 cups. Blend butter, flour and seasonings in saucepan. Stir in milk mixture gradually and cook over moderate heat until thick, stirring constantly. Mix half the sauce with spaghetti and mushrooms in a greased 2 quart casserole. Stir salmon into remaining sauce. Spoon into center of spaghetti and sprinkle with cheese and crumbs. Bake at 350 degrees for 30 minutes or until bubbly. Makes 4 servings.

Nutritional Analysis Per Serving:

Calories:. 360.5	Vitamin C:. . . . . .1 mg
Protein:. . . . . .29 g	Thiamine:. . . . . .2 mg
Carbohydrates:. . . . .24.75 g	Riboflavin:. . . . . .43 mg
Fat:. . . . . .15.5 g	Niacin:. . . . . .10.35 mg
Phosphate:. . . . . . . .446.5 mg	Calcium:. . . . . .336.75 mg
Potassium:. . . . . .582 mg	Iron:. . . . . .1.9 mg
Zinc:. . . . . .1.8 mg	Cholesterol:. . . . . .64.5 mg
Vitamin A:. . . . . . . .385.75 iu	Sodium. . . . . .632.75 mg

41

Salmon Quiche

½   onion, finely chopped
2   5.33 ounce cans evaporated milk
4   eggs, beaten
1   large can salmon
2   cups grated cheese
1   unbaked pie shell
     butter
     salt and pepper to taste

Saute onion in butter in skillet. Add evaporated milk, eggs, salmon, cheese, salt and pepper, mixing well. Pour into pie shell and bake at 375 degrees for 40 minutes. Makes 6 servings.

Nutritional Analysis Per Serving:

Calories: 559	Vitamin C: . . . . 1.83 mg
Protein: . . . . 33.67 g	Thiamine: . . . . .18 mg
Carbohydrates: . . . . . 19.83 g	Riboflavin: . . . . .6 mg
Fat: . . . . 38 g	Niacin: . . . . 6.9 mg
Phosphate: . . . . 581.67 mg	Calcium: . . . . 576.33 mg
Potassium: . . . . 527 mg	Iron: . . . . 2.13 mg
Zinc: . . . . 2.85 mg	Cholesterol: . . . . 255 mg
Vitamin A: . . . . 879.33 iu	Sodium: . . . . 837.33 mg

Baked Crab Casserole

4	tablespoons butter
4	tablespoons flour
2	cups milk
1/8	teaspoon pepper
½	teaspoon celery salt
1	egg yolk, beaten
2	tablespoons sherry
1	cup soft bread crumbs
1	pound crab meat
1	teaspoon minced parsley
1	teaspoon minced onion
½	cup buttered crumbs
	paprika to taste
	red pepper to taste

Melt butter. Add flour and blend. Add milk and seasonings gradually. Cook over low heat, stirring constantly, until thick. Add egg yolk gradually. Cook 2 minutes longer. Remove from heat. Add sherry, bread crumbs, crab meat, parsley and onion, mix well. Place in greased 1½ quart casserole. Top with buttered crumbs. Sprinkle with paprika. Bake at 400 degrees for 25 minutes. Makes 4 servings.

Nutritional Analysis Per Serving:

Calories:	354	Vitamin C:	2 mg
Protein:	19.5 g	Thiamine:	.27 mg
Carbohydrates:	25.25 g	Riboflavin.	.375 mg
Fat:	19.25 g	Niacin:	2.67 mg
Phosphate:	291.5 mg	Calcium:	212 mg
Potassium:	304.75 mg	Iron:	1.77 mg
Zinc:	3.22 mg	Cholesterol:	176.75 mg
Vitamin A:	1415 iu	Sodium:	1076.5 mg

Creamy Shrimp and Noodles

1	cup onion, finely chopped
½	cup green pepper, finely chopped
1	cup tomatoes, drained and finely chopped
1½	pounds shrimp, finely chopped
3	tablespoons margarine, melted
1	tablespoon paprika
¼	teaspoon pepper
1	cup sour cream
13	ounce package cream cheese, cubed
18	ounce package thin noodles, cooked and drained

Cook onion, green pepper, tomatoes and shrimp in margarine in large skillet over medium-low heat for 20 minutes, stirring occasionally. Add seasonings, sour cream and cream cheese, mixing well. Continue to cook until cream cheese is melted, stirring constantly. Do not boil. Stir in noodles. Makes 8 servings.

Nutritional Analysis Per Serving:

Calories:	*398*	*Vitamin C:*	*22 mg*
Protein:	*22.63 g*	*Thiamine:*	*.21 mg*
Carbohydrates:	*18.75 g*	*Riboflavin:*	*.25 mg*
Fat:	*26 g*	*Niacin:*	*4.08 mg*
Phosphate:	*259.5 mg*	*Calcium:*	*138.25 mg*
Potassium:	*435.63 mg*	*Iron:*	*2.75 mg*
Zinc:	*2.09 mg*	*Cholesterol:*	*204.5 mg*
Vitamin A:	*1371.88 iu*	*Sodium:*	*359.5 mg*

Shrimp Delight

1   green pepper, finely chopped
1   onion, finely chopped
1   stick margarine
2   cups rice
1   can cream of onion soup
1   can cream of celery soup
1½   pounds shrimp, very finely chopped

Saute green pepper and onion in margarine in skillet until tender. Stir in rice and soups. Add shrimp, mixing well. Spoon into lightly greased 9x13 inch casserole. Cover, and bake for 30 minutes at 350 degrees; stir and bake for additional 30 minutes covered. Makes 4 servings.

Nutritional Analysis Per Serving:

Calories:.........564.75	Vitamin C:............56 mg
Protein: ....38.25 g	Thiamine:............ .2 mg
Carbohydrates: .....36.25 g	Riboflavin: .... .175 mg
Fat: ....29 g	Niacin: ....6.55 mg
Phosphate: ....366.25 mg	Calcium:..........181.5 mg
Potassium:........660.25 mg	Iron: ....4.45 mg
Zinc: ....3.37 mg	Cholesterol: ....274.5 mg
Vitamin A: ....1254.5 iu	Sodium: ....1987.75 mg

Imperial Creamed Crab Meat

1	pound crab meat, cooked and flaked
2	tablespoons lemon juice
4	ounces cream cheese, softened
½	cup cream
3	green onions, finely chopped
¼	teaspoon dillweed
¼	cup parmesan cheese
¼	cup bread crumbs
2	tablespoons butter, melted
	salt and pepper to taste

Combine crab meat, lemon juice, cream cheese, cream, onions, dillweed, salt and pepper; blend well. Place crab mixture in casserole. Mix cheese, bread crumbs and butter in bowl. Sprinkle over casserole. Bake at 350 degrees for 15 minutes. Makes 6 servings.

Nutritional Analysis Per Serving:

Calories:...........252.5		Vitamin C:.............3 mg	
Protein:..............12 g		Thiamine:.......... .07 mg	
Carbohydrates:......5.33 g		Riboflavin: .... .13 mg	
Fat:................20.5 g		Niacin: ....1.1 mg	
Phosphate: ....156.33 mg		Calcium:...........113.5 mg	
Potassium:.........113.7 mg		Iron: .... .817 mg	
Zinc: ....1.93 mg		Cholesterol:.......107.66 mg	
Vitamin A: ....1233.17 iu		Sodium: ....660.5 mg	

Hot Crab-Avocado Casserole

¼   cup butter, melted
3   tablespoons flour
¼   teaspoon red pepper
¼   teaspoon thyme
2   cups milk
2   avocados
15   ounces crab meat, drained and flaked
½   cup parmesan cheese

Blend butter, flour and seasonings in saucepan adding milk gradually. Cook until thick, stirring constantly. Chop avocados and coat with lemon juice. Add crab meat, and avocado, mixing well. Place in large casserole and sprinkle with cheese. Broil for 2 minutes or until golden. Makes 6 servings.

Nutritional Analysis Per Serving:

Calories: 342		Vitamin C: .... 11.33 mg	
Protein: .... 15.67 g		Thiamine: .... .18 mg	
Carbohydrates: ..... 12.17 g		Riboflavin: .... .37 mg	
Fat: .... 26.83 g		Niacin: .... 2.33 mg	
Phosphate: .... 257.67 mg		Calcium: .... 243.67 mg	
Potassium: .... 642.5 mg		Iron: ... . 1.08 mg	
Zinc: .... 2.43 mg		Cholesterol: .... 81.17 mg	
Vitamin A: .... 1128.5 iu		Sodium: .... 761.83 mg	

Fillet of Sole Casserole

1½	pounds fillets of sole
2	ounces swiss cheese, shredded
¼	cup green onion, finely chopped
2	ounce can mushrooms, finely chopped
½	can cream of shrimp soup
½	teaspoon prepared mustard
1	teaspoon parsley, finely chopped
	pinch of cayenne pepper
	pinch of nutmeg
	salt and pepper to taste
	paprika

Arrange fillets over bottom of shallow 6x10 inch baking dish and cover with cheese and onion. Combine other ingredients, except paprika, in sauce pan, mixing well. Cook until heated through, stirring constantly. Pour over fillets. Sprinkle with paprika. Bake at 375 degrees for 20 minutes or until bubbly. Makes 6 servings.

Nutritional Analysis Per Serving:

Calories:	298.67	Vitamin C:	1 mg
Protein:	43.83 g	Thiamine:	.12 mg
Carbohydrates:	1.83 g	Riboflavin:	.21 mg
Fat:	11.67 g	Niacin:	4.5 mg
Phosphate:	458 mg	Calcium:	141.17 mg
Potassium:	617.33 mg	Iron:	1.56 mg
Zinc:	1.35 mg	Cholesterol:	126.33 mg
Vitamin A:	368.17 iu	Sodium:	348 mg

Kent's Seafood Casserole

1   can cream of shrimp soup
1   can cream of mushroom soup
2   cups white sauce
½   cup cheddar cheese, grated
1½ pounds fish fillets, baked and flaked
    crushed corn flakes

Combine all ingredients except corn flakes, in saucepan, mixing well. Simmer for several minutes. Pour into 9x13 inch casserole and top with corn flakes. Bake at 350 degrees for 20 minutes. Makes 6 servings.

Nutritional Analysis Per Serving:

Calories:............551.5	Vitamin C:.............3 mg
Protein: ....49.33 g	Thiamine:...........25 mg
Carbohydrates: .....18.67 g	Riboflavin: ....46 mg
Fat: ....30 g	Niacin. ....5.75 mg
Phosphate: ....557.66 mg	Calcium:..........240.67 mg
Potassium:........772.67 mg	Iron: ....2.317 mg
Zinc: ....2.2 mg	Cholesterol:.......172.67 mg
Vitamin A: ....1001.67 iu	Sodium: ....1416.83 mg

Cheddar Cod

4   cod cutlets
2   teaspoons lemon juice
2   tablespoons margarine
2   tablespoons flour
½   pint milk
½   cup cheddar cheese, grated
½   teaspoon mustard

Wash and dry the cod and place in a shallow ovenproof dish. Sprinkle with the lemon juice and salt and pepper to taste. Place the margarine, flour and milk in a pan. Heat, whisking until the sauce thickens. Continue cooking for 1 minute. Stir in cheese, mustard. Pour mixture over cod and bake at 350 degrees for 30 minutes. Makes 4 servings.

Nutritional Analysis Per Serving:

Calories:	1483.75 mg	Vitamin C:	1.75 mg
Protein:	31.75 g	Thiamine:	.15 mg
Carbohydrates:	7.75 g	Riboflavin:	.33 mg
Fat:	149 g	Niacin:	2.85 mg
Phosphate:	405.5 mg	Calcium:	253.5 mg
Potassium:	532.75 mg	Iron:	1.15 mg
Zinc:	1.13 mg	Cholesterol:	92.25 mg
Vitamin A:	6035 iu	Sodium:	1831.5 mg

Golden Shrimp Casserole

9   slices bread, trimmed and cubed
2   cups sharp cheddar cheese, grated
1½   pounds cooked shrimp, chopped into
            tiny pieces
4   ounce can mushrooms, chopped very fine
4   eggs
2¾   cups milk
¾   teaspoons dry mustard
½   teaspoon salt
1   can cream of shrimp soup

Place bread cubes in bottom of buttered 9x13 casserole and sprinkle cheese on top. Layer shrimp and mushrooms over cheese. Beat eggs, 2¼ cups milk, dry mustard and salt in bowl until well blended and pour over mushrooms. Cover and chill overnight. Blend soup and ½ cup milk; pour over casserole. Bake at 350 degrees for 1½ hours. Makes 8 servings.

Nutritional Analysis Per Serving:

Calories: 393.88	Vitamin C: . . . . 1.13 mg
Protein: . . . . 31.25 g	Thiamine: . . . . .02 mg
Carbohydrates: . . . . . 23.25 g	Riboflavin: . . . . .46 mg
Fat: . . . . 19 g	Niacin: . . . . 4.23 mg
Phosphate: . . . . 295.88 mg	Calcium: . . . . 406.75 mg
Potassium: . . . . 453.75 mg	Iron: . . . . 3.01 mg
Zinc: . . . . 325.13 mg	Cholesterol: . . . . 295.75 mg
Vitamin A: . . . . 542.5 iu	Sodium: . . . . 973.25 mg

Shrimp and Mushroom Casserole

1   pound boiled shrimp, chopped very fine
2   cans cream of mushroom soup
1   cup mayonnaise
2   pimentos, finely chopped
1   clove of garlic, minced
2   teaspoons worcestershire sauce
2   hard-boiled eggs, finely chopped
½   cups bread crumbs
       salt and pepper to taste

Combine all ingredients except bread crumbs in bowl, mixing well. Spoon into lightly greased 3 quart casserole. Sprinkle bread crumbs over casserole. Bake at 350 degrees for 20 minutes. Makes 6 servings.

Nutritional Analysis Per Serving:

Calories:..........500.33	Vitamin C: ....2.33 mg
Protein:..............18 g	Thiamine:...........06 mg
Carbohydrates:........17 g	Riboflavin:...........2 mg
Fat:...............40.17 g	Niacin: ....3.26 mg
Phosphate: ....208.83 mg	Calcium:..........107.33 mg
Potassium:........300.17 mg	Iron: ....2.45 mg
Zinc: ....1.83 mg	Cholesterol:........216.5 mg
Vitamin A: ....300.66 iu	Sodium:............1226 mg

Baked Shrimp-Cheese Puff

4	slices buttered bread, cut into ½ inch cubes
½	pound shrimp, chopped into very tiny pieces
½	pound cheese, grated
3	eggs, beaten
2	cups milk
¼	teaspoon dry mustard
	salt and pepper to taste

Layer bread, shrimp and cheese alternately in buttered 1½ quart casserole. Combine eggs, milk and seasonings in bowl, beating well. Pour over casserole and top with additional cheese. Bake at 350 degrees for 45 minutes. Makes 6 servings.

Nutritional Analysis Per Serving:

Calories:	368.5	Vitamin C:	.83 mg
Protein:	24 g	Thiamine:	.13 mg
Carbohydrates:	13.67 g	Riboflavin:	.4 mg
Fat:	24 g	Niacin:	2.05 mg
Phosphate:	397.5 mg	Calcium:	423.67 mg
Potassium:	303 mg	Iron:	1.93 mg
Zinc:	2.55 mg	Cholesterol:	253 mg
Vitamin A:	822.5 iu	Sodium:	504 mg

Lobster and Mushroom Casserole

1   pound mushrooms, finely chopped
4   tablespoons butter
3   tablespoons flour
        dash of pepper
1½   cups milk
½   cup chicken broth
2   cups lobster, finely chopped
2   egg yolks
½   cups cream
        bread crumbs

Saute mushrooms in butter for 5 minutes. Add flour, and pepper, stir in milk and broth gradually and cook until thick, stirring constantly. Add lobster, mixing well. Beat egg yolks with cream in bowl and stir into lobster mixture. Cook over low heat until heated, stirring frequently. Pour into lightly buttered casserole, sprinkle with bread crumbs. Bake at 450 degrees for 10 minutes. Makes 6 servings.

Nutritional Analysis Per Serving:

Calories:..........266.33	Vitamin C: ....1.5 mg
Protein: ....11.17 g	Thiamine:.......... .167 mg
Carbohydrates: .....19.33 g	Riboflavin: .... .33 mg
Fat:...............16.17 g	Niacin: ....2.4 mg
Phosphate: ....197.5 mg	Calcium:..........134.83 mg
Potassium: ....284 mg	Iron: ....1.43 mg
Zinc: ....1.38 mg	Cholesterol:.......148.67 mg
Vitamin A: ....605.67 iu	Sodium: ....417.17 mg

Seafood Quiche

¾   cup crab meat
¾   cup shrimp, cooked and finely chopped
1   cup swiss cheese, grated
⅓   cup celery, cooked and finely chopped
⅓   cup green onion, finely chopped
2   9 inch unbaked pie shells
⅔   cup mayonnaise
¼   cup flour
1   cup milk
6   eggs, slightly beaten

Combine crabmeat, shrimp, swiss cheese, celery and green onions in bowl, mix well. Divide in half. Place in 2 pie shells. Combine mayonnaise, flour, milk, and eggs in bowl, mix well. Divide in half. Pour over seafood mixture. Bake at 375 degrees for 30 minutes. Makes 8 servings.

Nutritional Analysis Per Serving:

Calories:.......... 531.5	Vitamin C .... 1.75 mg
Protein: .... 18.63 g	Thiamine:........... .23 mg
Carbohydrates: ...... 26.5 g	Riboflavin .... .34 mg
Fat: .... 38.87 g	Niacin: .. .. 2.5 mg
Phosphate: .... 267.25 mg	Calcium:.......... 224.25 mg
Potassium: .... 229 mg	Iron: .... 2.23 mg
Zinc: .... 2.23 mg	Cholesterol:....... 257.75 mg
Vitamin A: .... 537.88 iu	Sodium: .... 642.5 mg

Seafood Casserole

1   4 ounce small shrimp, drained, finely chopped
1   6½ ounce can crab meat, finely flaked
1   cup celery, finely chopped
1   cup onion, finely chopped
1   cup green pepper, minced
1   cup mayonnaise
     salt and pepper to taste
1   tablespoon worcestershire sauce
½   cup milk
1   cup buttered herb stuffing mix

Combine first nine ingredients and ¾ cup stuffing mix in bowl, mixing well. Spoon into buttered baking dish. Top with remaining stuffing mix. Bake at 350 degrees for 30 minutes. Makes 4 servings.

Nutritional Analysis Per Serving:

Calories:	550	Vitamin C:	59 mg
Protein:	11 g	Thiamine:	.18 mg
Carbohydrates:	23 g	Riboflavin:	.2 mg
Fat:	47 g	Niacin:	1.35 mg
Phosphate:	148.5 mg	Calcium:	114.5 mg
Potassium:	431 mg	Iron:	1.73 mg
Zinc:	1.55 mg	Cholesterol:	72.5 mg
Vitamin A:	769 iu	Sodium:	958 mg

Ham with Sweet Potatoes

1	egg
½	cup milk
1½	cups soft bread crumbs
2	cups cooked ham, twice ground
1	teaspoon dry mustard
1	pound can sweet potatoes
2	tablespoons melted butter
½	cup honey
2	tablespoons vinegar

In a bowl beat the egg slightly. Stir in the milk, bread crumbs, ground ham, and ½ teaspoon of the mustard. Mix lightly until well blended, then shape into about 12 balls. Distribute balls in a greased shallow baking dish. Arrange the sweet potatoes between the ham balls in the dish. Combine the melted butter, honey, vinegar, and remaining ½ teaspoon mustard; drizzle over the ham and pototoes. Bake, uncovered, in a 375 degree oven for 40 minutes. Makes 4 servings.

Nutritional Analysis Per Serving:

Calories:	560.5	Vitamin C:	10 mg
Protein:	38.5 g	Thiamine:	85 mg
Carbohydrates:	68.75 g	Riboflavin:	5 mg
Fat:	14.25 g	Niacin:	7.73 mg
Phosphate:	451.75 mg	Calcium:	108.5 mg
Potassium:	699 mg	Iron:	6.75 mg
Zinc:	5.1 mg	Cholesterol:	166 mg
Vitamin A:	6097 iu	Sodium:	250.25 mg

Ham-Potato Bake

1½   cups finely chopped ham
1   can cream of mushroom soup
¼   cup milk
1   tablespoon instant minced onion
1/8   teaspoon pepper
1   cup sharp American cheese, shredded
4   cups potatoes, cooked and finely diced
1   cup carrots, finely shredded
¾   cup soft bread crumbs
1   tablespoon butter, melted

Combine ham, cream of mushroom soup, milk, minced onion, pepper and ½ cup cheese, mixing well. Layer potatoes, carrots and ham mixture in 2 quart baking dish. Mix bread crumbs, remaining ½ cup cheese and butter and sprinkle over mixture. Bake at 350 for 45 minutes. Garnish with sprigs of parsley. Makes 6 servings.

Nutritional Analysis Per Serving:

Calories:. 396.5	Vitamin C: . . . . .30.67 mg
Protein: . . . . .24 g	Thiamine:. . . . . .55 mg
Carbohydrates:. . . . . . . .36 g	Riboflavin: . . . . .33 mg
Fat:. . . . . .17.5 g	Niacin: . . . . .5.33 mg
Phosphate: . . . . . .373.67 mg	Calcium: . . . . .175 mg
Potassium:. . . . . . .838.17 mg	Iron: . . . . .3.28 mg
Zinc: . . . . .3.77 mg	Cholesterol:. . . . . . . .78.17 mg
Vitamin A:. . . . . .2360 iu	Sodium: . . . . .1244.17 mg

Deviled Ham

2 cups diced cooked ham
2 tablespoons mayonnaise
1½ tablespoons dijon mustard
¼ teaspoon tabasco

Process ham in food processor or blender until smooth paste is formed. Add mayonnaise, mustard and tabasco. Process until blended. Makes 1½ cups.

Nutritional Analysis Per Serving:

Calories:	271.33	Vitamin C:	0 mg
Protein:	12.17 g	Thiamine:	.25 mg
Carbohydrates:	1.33 g	Riboflavin:	.17 mg
Fat:	23.83 g	Niacin.	2.4 mg
Phosphate:	90.33 mg	Calcium:	11.16 mg
Potassium:	184 mg	Iron:	1.87 mg
Zinc:	234.33 mg	Cholesterol:	73.83 mg
Vitamin A:	13 iu	Sodium:	1060.5 mg

Egg - Beef - Spinach Treat

2	pounds lean beef, twice ground
2	tablespoons olive oil
2	onions, finely chopped
2	cloves garlic, mashed
½	pound mushrooms, finely chopped
¼	teaspoon ground nutmeg
¼	teaspoon pepper
¼	teaspoon oregano
10	ounce package frozen chopped spinach
4	eggs

Brown ground beef well in oil in a large frying pan over high heat. Add onions, garlic, and mushrooms; reduce heat and continue cooking, stirring occasionally, until onion is soft. Stir in nutmeg, pepper, oregano, and spinach; cook about 5 minutes longer. Add eggs; stir mixture over low heat just until eggs begin to set. Makes 6 servings.

Nutritional Analysis Per Serving:

Calories:	362	Vitamin C:	11.33 mg
Protein:	36.83 g	Thiamine:	.2 mg
Carbohydrates:	5.17 g	Riboflavin:	.48 mg
Fat:	21 g	Niacin:	7.57 mg
Phosphate:	359.83 mg	Calcium:	92.5 mg
Potassium:	623.33 mg	Iron:	5.77 mg
Zinc:	6.88 mg	Cholesterol:	270.83 mg
Vitamin A:	3569.17 iu	Sodium:	224.92 mg

Cottage Cheese Meat Loaf

1   pound lean beef, twice ground
1   cup cottage cheese
1   egg
½   cup quick-cooking rolled oats
¼   cup catsup
1   tablespoon prepared mustard
2   tablespoons onion, finely chopped
1/8   teaspoon pepper
⅓   cup grated parmesan cheese

Combine the ground beef with the cottage cheese, egg, rolled oats, catsup, prepared mustard, onion, and pepper. Mix the ingredients until well blended. Press the mixture loosely into a shallow baking pan. Bake, uncovered, in a 350 degree oven for 20 minutes. Remove and sprinkle with the parmesan cheese evenly over the top. Bake for another 10 minutes. Let stand for about 5 minutes before serving. Makes 4 servings.

Nutritional Analysis Per Serving:

Calories:...........356.5	Vitamin C:.............3 mg
Protein: ....36.75 g	Thiamine:........... .18 mg
Carbohydrates:........13 g	Riboflavin: ....38 mg
Fat:...............16.75 g	Niacin: ....5.55 mg
Phosphate: ....406.75 mg	Calcium:...........178.5 mg
Potassium:.........431.5 mg	Iron:.................4 mg
Zinc: ....5.45 mg	Cholesterol: ....156 mg
Vitamin A:...........432 iu	Sodium: ....569.63 mg

BBQ Meat Loaf

2   cups bread crumbs
½   cup onion, minced
1   tablespoon horseradish
2   teaspoons celery salt
2   teaspoons liquid smoke
1   teaspoon garlic salt
¼   teaspoon pepper
2   eggs
1½   pounds hamburger, twice ground
½   cup BBQ sauce

Combine bread crumbs, onions, 2 tablespoons water, horseradish, celery salt, liquid smoke, garlic salt, pepper and eggs. Add beef and mix well. Place in loaf pan and bake at 350 degrees for 30 minutes. Pour off grease. Pour on BBQ sauce and continue baking for 45 minutes. Adding more sauce if desired. Makes 8 servings.

Nutritional Analysis Per Serving:

Calories:	255.88	Vitamin C:	1.87 mg
Protein:	21.5 g	Thiamine:	.18 mg
Carbohydrates:	15.12 g	Riboflavin:	.25 mg
Fat:	23.25 g	Niacin:	5.13 mg
Phosphate:	214.75 mg	Calcium:	44.75 mg
Potassium:	370.63 mg	Iron:	3.68 mg
Zinc:	3.93 mg	Cholesterol:	120 mg
Vitamin A:	135.88 iu	Sodium:	333.5 mg

Hamburger - Greenbean Casserole

1   pound hamburger, twice ground
1   onion, finely chopped
¼   teaspoon pepper
1   can tomato soup
1   16 ounce can greenbeans, drained
4   slices American cheese
1   5 ounce box instant mashed potatoes

Brown hamburger and onion in large skillet. Add pepper. Mix hamburger with tomato soup. Place in 2 quart casserole. Place green beans on top. Prepare instant mashed potatoes according to package directions for 6 servings. Spread over green beans. Top with cheese. Bake at 350 degrees for 30 minutes. Makes 6 servings.

Nutritional Analysis Per Serving:

Calories:.........342.33	Vitamin C: ....12.5 mg
Protein: ....23.17 g	Thiamine:..............15 mg
Carbohydrates: .....23.67 g	Riboflavin: ....28 mg
Fat: ....17.33 g	Niacin: ....5.18 mg
Phosphate: ....362.17 mg	Calcium:..........194.16 mg
Potassium: ....715 mg	Iron: ....3.7 mg
Zinc: ....4.37 mg	Cholesterol:........82.33 mg
Vitamin A: ....80.95 iu	Sodium: ....939.33 mg

Hamburger Stew

1   pound hamburger, twice ground
1   teaspoon garlic salt
1   cup cabbage, finely shredded
2   teaspoons shortening
1   cup cooked carrots, shredded
1   cup cooked potatoes, shredded
2   cups barbecue sauce
2   16 ounce cans pork and beans

Brown beef and garlic salt in skillet. Cook cabbage in 2 cups water and shortening until tender in large saucepan. Add beef and remaining ingredients. Bring to a boil Reduce heat. Let simmer for 30 minutes. Makes 8 servings.

Nutritional Analysis Per Serving:

Calories: 363		Vitamin C: . . . . 21.38 mg	
Protein: . . . . 21.63 g		Thiamine: . . . . .21 mg	
Carbohydrates: . . . . . 37.88 g		Riboflavin: . . . . .18 mg	
Fat: . . . . 14.50 g		Niacin: . . . . 4.50 mg	
Phosphate: . . . . 268.13 mg		Calcium: . . . . 106.88 mg	
Potassium: . . . . 792.38 mg		Iron: . . . . 4.95 mg	
Zinc: . . . . 4.86 mg		Cholesterol: . . . . 43.50 mg	
Vitamin A: . . . . 2398.38 iu		Sodium: . . . . 1150.63 mg	

Tuna Vegetable Potato Topper

2   tablespoons chopped onion
3   tablespoons chopped green pepper
2   tablespoons unsalted butter
1½   tablespoons all-purpose flour
¼   teaspoon onion powder
¼   teaspoon garlic powder
1/8   teaspoon ground thyme
1   cup milk
2   tablespoons dairy sour cream
½   cup thinly sliced carrots, cooked and drained
6½   ounces of light tuna, drained
4   baking potatoes, baked
      dash ground marjoram

In a medium-size saucepan saute onion and green pepper in butter about 3 minutes or until onion is tender. Combine flour, onion powder, garlic powder, thyme and marjoram. Stir into onion mixture. Heat and stir until bubbly. Remove from heat. Slowly stir in milk and cream. Heat and stir until sauce just comes to a boil and is thickened. Stir in carrots and tuna. Heat through or until carrots are soft. Serve over split baked potatoes. Makes 4 servings.

Nutritional Analysis Per Serving:

Calories:.........354.25	Vitamin C:............52 mg
Protein: ....18.75 g	Thiamine:...........28 mg
Carbohydrates: .....49.75 g	Riboflavin: ....25 mg
Fat:................9.5 g	Niacin: ....8.75 mg
Phosphate: ....276.75 mg	Calcium:.........114.25 mg
Potassium:.......1281.75 mg	Iron: ....2.35 mg
Zinc: ....1.33 mg	Cholesterol: ....50 mg
Vitamin A: ....2375.5 iu	Sodium:.............65 mg

Dane's Tuna Casserole

1	12½ ounce can tuna, finely flaked
1	cup cooked rice
1	small onion, minced
1	egg beaten
	juice of ½ lemon
1	cup celery, very finely chopped
½	cup green pepper, very finely chopped
1	can cream of mushroom soup
1	cup parmesan cheese

Combine all ingredients, except parmesan cheese, in bowl, mixing well. Spoon into lightly greased baking dish. Sprinkle parmesan cheese over top. Bake at 350 degrees for 35 minutes. Makes 4 servings.

Nutritional Analysis Per Serving:

Calories:.........373.75		Vitamin C:............14 mg	
Protein: ....36.25 g		Thiamine:.......... .17 mg	
Carbohydrates:........23 g		Riboflavin: .... .32 mg	
Fat: ....15 g		Niacin: ....11.2 mg	
Phosphate: ....431.75 mg		Calcium:..........417.75 mg	
Potassium: ....553 mg		Iron: ....2.75 mg	
Zinc: ....2.3 mg		Cholesterol: ....134 mg	
Vitamin A: ....538.75 iu		Sodium:............1260 mg	

Tuna Casserole

8   ounce package small macaroni, cooked
¼   green pepper, finely chopped
1   can tomato soup
6   ounces evaporated milk
1   6½ ounce can light chunk tuna, finely chopped
8   ounces cheddar cheese, grated

Mix first 5 ingredients and half the cheese with ½ milk can of water in 2 quart casserole. Sprinkle remaining cheese over top. Bake at 350 degrees for 40 minutes. Makes 4 servings.

Nutritional Analysis Per Serving:

Calories:..........601.5		Vitamin C:............18 mg
Protein: ....35.75 g		Thiamine:.............37 mg
Carbohydrates: .....59.25 g		Riboflavin: ....6 mg
Fat:...............24.25 g		Niacin: ....7.87 mg
Phosphate: ....574.25 mg		Calcium: ....559 mg
Potassium: ....525 mg		Iron: .. ..3.27 mg
Zinc: ....3.6 mg		Cholesterol:.........96.5 mg
Vitamin A: 1103.75iu		Sodium: 722.75mg

Tuna Spread

1   7 ounce can tuna, drained
⅓   cup mayonnaise
2   parsley sprigs
1   green onion, cut in pieces
      juice of ½ lemon
      salt and pepper to taste

Process all ingredients in food processor or blender until evenly mixed. Makes 1 cup.

Nutritional Analysis Per Serving:

Calories:.......... 232.75	Vitamin C:............. 4 mg
Protein: .... 14.75 g	Thiamine:........... .03 mg
Carbohydrates:........ 1 g	Riboflavin: .... .05 mg
Fat:............... 18.75 g	Niacin: .... 5.98 mg
Phosphate: .... 123 mg	Calcium:............ 8.75 mg
Potassium:....... 170.74 mg	Iron: .... 1.1 mg
Zinc: .... 58 mg	Cholesterol:........ 43.25 mg
Vitamin A: .... 135.5 iu	Sodium: .... 505.25 mg

Tuna Pate

1   10 ounce can tuna, drained
1   cup softened butter
3   drops lemon juice
3   drops tabasco
10   medium shrimp, cooked and shelled
3   tablespoons pimentos, finely chopped

Add tuna, butter, lemon juice, tabasco, salt and pepper to food processor or blender. Process until smooth. Add shrimp and pimentos. Process until ingredients are evenly chopped and combined. Pack the pate into a well oiled 3 cup loaf pan or mold and chill for 24 hours. Makes 6 servings.

Nutritional Analysis Per Serving:

Calories:	360	Vitamin C:	9 mg
Protein:	14.17 g	Thiamine:	.03 mg
Carbohydrates:	1 g	Riboflavin:	.06 mg
Fat:	33.66 g	Niacin:	4.73 mg
Phosphate:	128.83 mg	Calcium:	35 mg
Potassium:	181.33 mg	Iron:	1.22 mg
Zinc:	.07 mg	Cholesterol:	138.5 mg
Vitamin A:	1468.67 iu	Sodium:	613.5 mg

Turkey Patties

1½ pounds turkey, twice ground
¼ cup fine dry bread crumbs
1 egg
2 tablespoons mushrooms, finely chopped
2 tablespoons green onion, finely chopped
2 garlic cloves, crushed
1½ teaspoons ground ginger
2½ tablespoons soy sauce

Mix all ingredients together. Shape into six patties. Place in boiler pan about four inches from heat and cook 5 minutes on each side. Makes 6 servings.

Nutritional Analysis Per Serving:

Calories:............226.5	Vitamin C: ....5 mg
Protein: ....35.17 g	Thiamine:...........1 mg
Carbohydrates:.........4 g	Riboflavin: ....27 mg
Fat:................6.83 g	Niacin: ....6.42 mg
Phosphate: ....270.83 mg	Calcium:...........44.33 mg
Potassium:........391.83 mg	Iron: ....2.73 mg
Zinc: ....3.7 mg	Cholesterol:.......127.33 mg
Vitamin A:...........39 iu	Sodium: ....668.67 mg

Curried Turkey

2 16 ounce packages frozen chopped broccoli, thawed, drained
8 cups turkey, cooked, chopped fine in blender
1 can cream of chicken soup
1 can cream of celery soup
1 can cream of mushroom soup
1 cup milk
1 cup mayonnaise
2 teaspoons curry
1 tablespoons lemon juice
1 pound mild cheddar cheese, grated

Layer broccoli and turkey in large, lightly buttered, baking dish. Blend remaining ingredients, except cheese, in a bowl. Pour over turkey. Sprinkle top with cheese. Cover and bake at 350 degrees for 1 hour. (Note) Yields approximately 20 servings.

Nutritional Analysis Per Serving:

Calories:	381	Vitamin C:	21.55 mg
Protein:	34.55 g	Thiamine:	.10 mg
Carbohydrates:	6.3 g	Riboflavin:	.34 mg
Fat:	23.9 g	Niacin:	5.26 mg
Phosphate:	357.8 mg	Calcium:	234.85 mg
Potassium:	429.3 mg	Iron:	2.295 mg
Zinc:	3.84 mg	Cholesterol:	103.9 mg
Vitamin A:	1330.15 iu	Sodium:	637.6 mg

Turkey Amandzine

¾   cup mayonnaise
⅓   cup flour
2   tablespoons minced onion
1   teaspoon garlic salt
2¼   cups milk
1   cup swiss cheese, shredded
7   ounces spaghetti, cooked, drained and
        finely chopped
2   cups turkey, finely chopped in blender
10   ounces frozen broccoli, thawed, drained and
        finely chopped
¼   cup chopped pimento
1   can cream of mushroom soup

Blend mayonnaise, flour, minced onion and garlic salt in medium saucepan. Add milk and cook over slow heat until thick; stirring constantly. Stir in cheese until cheese is melted. Add remaining ingredients and mix well. Spoon into 8x12 inch baking dish. Bake at 350 degrees for 45 minutes. Makes 6 servings.

Nutritional Analysis Per Serving:

Calories:. 654.17	Vitamin C: . . . . .32.16 mg
Protein: . . . . .37 g	Thiamine:. . . . . .3 mg
Carbohydrates: . . . . .39.17 g	Riboflavin: . . . . .55 mg
Fat: . . . . .38.83 g	Niacin: . . . . .6.12 mg
Phosphate: . . . . . . .465.83 mg	Calcium:. . . . . .370.5 mg
Potassium:. . . . . . . .606.66 mg	Iron: . . . . .3.3 mg
Zinc: . . . . .4.33 mg	Cholesterol: . . . . .108 mg
Vitamin A: . . . . . . .1605.33 iu	Sodium: . . . . .713.33 mg

Chicken Casserole

6   cooked chicken breasts, finely chopped
2   cups sour cream
2   cups mushroom soup
1   teaspoon worcestershire sauce
1   4 ounce can mushrooms, drained and finely chopped
1   6 ounce box stuffing mix

Place chicken in bottom of buttered casserole. Mix sour cream, soup, worcestershire sauce and mushrooms. Pour over chicken. Prepare stuffing mix according to package directions; cool. Spread over casserole. Bake uncovered at 350 degrees for 30 minutes. Makes 8 servings.

Nutritional Analysis Per Serving:

Calories: 322	Vitamin C: . . . . .1.5 mg
Protein: . . . . .24.25 g	Thiamine: . . . . .175 mg
Carbohydrates: . . . . .19.37 g	Riboflavin: . . . . .27 mg
Fat: . . . . .16.12 g	Niacin: . . . . .8.64 mg
Phosphate: . . . . . . .205.75 mg	Calcium: . . . . .94.5 mg
Potassium: . . . . .315.13 mg	Iron: . . . . .1.2 mg
Zinc: . . . . .1.35 mg	Cholesterol: . . . . .77.88 mg
Vitamin A: . . . . .421.62 iu	Sodium: . . . . .673.63 mg

Easy Chicken Treat

3   cups cooked chicken, finely chopped in blender
2   cups milk
1   can cream of chicken soup
1   can cream of mushroom soup
1   small onion, minced
1   cup Velveeta cheese, diced
½   cup green pepper, minced
½   cup celery, very finely chopped

Combine all ingredients in baking dish, cover and chill overnight. Bake at 350 degrees for 1 hour. Makes 4 servings.

Nutritional Analysis Per Serving:

Calories:.........514.25	Vitamin C: ....30.25 mg
Protein: ....35.5 g	Thiamine:............18 mg
Carbohydrates: .....25.25 g	Riboflavin: ....68 mg
Fat: ....30.25 g	Niacin: ....6.9 mg
Phosphate: ....704 mg	Calcium:.........523.75 mg
Potassium:........712.75 mg	Iron: ....1.95 mg
Zinc: ....4.08 mg	Cholesterol: ....116 mg
Vitamin A:..........1062 iu	Sodium:...........2094 mg

74

The Slick Chick

1   can cream of mushroom soup
1   can cream of chicken soup
½   cup milk
½   teaspoon onion powder
4   cups rice, cooked
3   cups chicken, finely chopped in blender
1   cup cheddar cheese, grated
2   tablespoons pimento, finely chopped

Combine soups and milk in large saucepan, mixing well, while heating and stirring constantly. When heated add all remaining ingredients and heat. Pour into a lightly greased 2 quart casserole. Bake at 375 for 30 minutes. Makes 6 servings.

Nutritional Analysis Per Serving:

Calories:	449.67	Vitamin C:	9.17 mg
Protein:	30.33 g	Thiamine:	.22 mg
Carbohydrates:	38.33 g	Riboflavin:	.32 mg
Fat:	18.67 g	Niacin:	8.22 mg
Phosphate:	322 mg	Calcium:	218.66 mg
Potassium:	348.5 mg	Iron:	2.62 mg
Zinc:	3.12 mg	Cholesterol:	92.83 mg
Vitamin A:	680.67 iu	Sodium:	991.5 mg

Holiday Chicken Casserole

6   ounce package noodles, cooked
1   can cream of chicken soup
6   ounce can evaporated milk
1½   cups American cheese, shredded
2   cups chicken, cooked and finely chopped
      in blender
1   cup celery, very finely chopped
¼   cup green pepper, very finely chopped
¼   cup pimento, finely chopped

Spread noodles over bottom and up sides of 2 quart casserole. Combine soup, evaporated milk in saucepan and heat, stirring constantly. When heated add cheese until cheese melts, continue to stir. Stir in remaining ingredients, after well mixed, pour over noodles. Bake at 350 degrees for 30 minutes. Makes 4 servings.

Nutritional Analysis Per Serving:

Calories:.........626.25	Vitamin C:............30 mg
Protein:.............45 g	Thiamine:...........33 mg
Carbohydrates:......45.5 g	Riboflavin:..........63 mg
Fat: ....29 g	Niacin: ....10.05 mg
Phosphate: ....692.75 mg	Calcium: ....456 mg
Potassium:........682.75 mg	Iron: ....3.2 mg
Zinc: ....4.8 mg	Cholesterol:........177.5 mg
Vitamin A: ....1475.75 iu	Sodium: ....1476.5 mg

Chicken Encore

14 ounces cooked chicken, finely chopped in blender
8 ounce of elbow macaroni, very small
2 cans cream of mushroom soup
4 hard boiled eggs, finely chopped
1 medium onion, minced
1 cup milk
1 cup chicken broth
½ pound mild cheese, cubed

Combine all ingredients in 9x13 inch baking dish, mixing well. Cover and chill overnight. Bake at 350 degrees for 1 hour. Makes 4 servings.

Nutritional Analysis Per Serving:

Calories:...........1076.5		Vitamin C: ....4.75 mg
Protein: ....70 g		Thiamine:.............43 mg
Carbohydrates: .....57.75 g		Riboflavin: ....1.08 mg
Fat:...............62.25 g		Niacin: ....11.95 mg
Phosphate: ......1325.25 mg		Calcium:..........883.75 mg
Potassium:........857.75 mg		Iron: ....4.85 mg
Zinc: ....7.93 mg		Cholesterol:........454.5 mg
Vitamin A: ....1831.25 iu		Sodium: ....3358.75 mg

Velveeta Chicken

1   6 ounce box chicken-flavored stuffing mix
1   can cream of chicken soup
6   ounces Velveeta cheese
6   ounces evaporated milk
1   chicken, baked, boned and finely chopped
     in blender

Prepare stuffing mix using package directions. Combine cream of chicken soup, Velveeta cheese and milk. Cook over low heat until cheese melts. Layer chicken, cheese mixture and stuffing in 9x11 casserole and bake 30 minutes at 350 degrees. Makes 6 servings.

Nutritional Analysis Per Serving:

Calories:	631.83	Vitamin C:	1.17 mg
Protein:	74.17 g	Thiamine:	.25 mg
Carbohydrates:	17.33 g	Riboflavin:	68.5 mg
Fat:	27.83 g	Niacin:	4.43 mg
Phosphate:	718.5 mg	Calcium:	293.67 mg
Potassium:	762 mg	Iron:	3.18 mg
Zinc:	6.03 mg	Cholesterol:	228.33 mg
Vitamin A:	588.17 iu	Sodium:	1187.17 mg

Baked Chicken Salad

1   cup potato chips, finely crushed
⅔   cup sharp cheddar cheese, shredded
4   cups chicken, cooked and finely chopped
2   cups celery, finely chopped
2   tablespoons onion, finely chopped
½   cup almonds, minced
¾   cup mayonnaise
1   can cream of chicken soup
2   tablespoons lemon juice
2   pimentos, finely chopped
4   hard-boiled eggs, finely chopped

Mix potato chips and cheese in bowl. Combine the cheese mixture with the next nine ingredients, mixing well. Spoon into 1½ quart baking dish. Sprinkle eggs on top along with remaining cheese mixture. Chill for several hours. Bake at 400 degrees for 25 minutes. Serve hot. Makes 6 servings.

Nutritional Analysis Per Serving:

Calories:...........954.5		Vitamin C: ....16.5 *mg*	
Protein: ....57.33 *g*		Thiamine:.............28 *mg*	
Carbohydrates: .....29.33 *g*		Riboflavin: ....63 *mg*	
Fat:...............68.17 *g*		Niacin: ....16.62 *mg*	
Phosphate: ....590.17 *mg*		Calcium:..........226.33 *mg*	
Potassium:.......1180.83 *mg*		Iron: ....4.6 *mg*	
Zinc:...............5.08 *mg*		Cholesterol:.......326.67 *mg*	
Vitamin A:...........831 *iu*		Sodium: ....937.5 *mg*	

Chicken and Rice

1½   cups minute rice
1   can cream of mushroom soup
1   can cream of celery soup
1   cup milk
8   chicken breasts, skinned and chopped
        in blender
½   package dry onion soup mix

Mix rice, cream of mushroom soup, cream of celery soup and milk in 9x13 inch casserole. Layer chicken and dry onion soup mix over rice mixture. Bake tightly covered for 2 hours at 350 degrees. Makes 8 servings.

Nutritional Analysis Per Serving:

Calories:..........267.88	Vitamin C: ....5 mg
Protein: ....29 g	Thiamine:.............13 mg
Carbohydrates:........15 g	Riboflavin: ....2 mg
Fat:.................9.5 g	Niacin: ....10.98 mg
Phosphate: ....243.25 mg	Calcium:...........78.25 mg
Potassium:........322.13 mg	Iron: ....1.51 mg
Zinc: ....1.44 mg	Cholesterol:........81.88 mg
Vitamin A: ....145.38 iu	Sodium: ....719.63 mg

Chicken Liver
and Avocado Spread

1   pound chicken livers
¼   cup butter
1   large avocado, peeled and cut into pieces
6   scallions, white part only, cut into pieces
½   cup softened butter
1½   teaspoons salt
1/8   teaspoon black pepper

Saute chicken livers in the ¼ cup butter over medium-high heat until livers are brown on outside, but still red and juicy inside. Add the chicken livers, avocado and scallions to food processor or blender. Process until a smooth paste is formed. Add softened butter, salt and pepper. Process until well mixed. Transfer to serving bowl. Place plastic wrap directly on spread to prevent discoloring. Cover bowl with additional plastic wrap to make an airtight seal. Refrigerate 4 hours. Makes 3 cups.

Nutritional Analysis Per Serving:

Calories:........... 147.5		Vitamin C: .... 7.44 mg
Protein: .... 6.63 g		Thiamine:........... .06 mg
Carbohydrates: ...... 1.69 g		Riboflavin: .... .48 mg
Fat: .... 1.25 g		Niacin: .... 1.43 mg
Phosphate: .... 89.69 mg		Calcium:........... 10.75 mg
Potassium:........ 153.56 mg		Iron: .... 2.28 mg
Zinc: .... .94 mg		Cholesterol: .... 181 mg
Vitamin A: .... 4470.56 iu		Sodium: .... 319.63 mg

Macaroni Souffle

½   cup elbow macaroni, cooked
1   4 ounce can mushrooms, drained and
         finely chopped
1   cup milk
3   egg yolks
½   onion
3   tablespoons all-purpose flour
1   cup sharp American cheese, cut in cubes
3   egg whites
¼   teaspoon cream of tartar

Put macaroni and enough water to cover in blender; blend until finely chopped. Drain; pour into saucepan. Add mushrooms. Put next five ingredients in blender; blend until smooth, add cheese. Pour over macaroni. Cook and stir until mixture thickens. Beat egg whites with cream of tartar to stiff peaks. Fold into macaroni. Bake for 50 minutes at 325 degrees. Makes 2 servings.

Nutritional Analysis Per Serving:

Calories:	528	Vitamin C:	4 mg
Protein:	29.5 g	Thiamine:	.3 mg
Carbohydrates:	35.5 g	Riboflavin:	.85 mg
Fat:	29.5 g	Niacin:	2.7 mg
Phosphate:	740.5 mg	Calcium:	549 mg
Potassium:	537.5 mg	Iron:	2.95 mg
Zinc:	4 mg	Cholesterol:	430.5 mg
Vitamin A:	1261.5 iu	Sodium:	1147.5 mg

82

Baked Eggs

6   eggs
1   package bread crumbs, about 2 cups
1   cup cheddar cheese, grated

Break eggs into buttered 6x8 inch baking dish, taking care not to break egg yolks. Sprinkle bread crumbs around outer edge of baking dish. Top with cheese. Bake at 350 degrees for 15 minutes or until eggs are set. Makes 2 servings.

Nutritional Analysis Per Serving:

Calories:.......... 636.5	Vitamin C:............. 0 mg
Protein:.............. 39 g	Thiamine:........... .55 mg
Carbohydrates:...... 42.5 g	Riboflavin:............. 1 mg
Fat:................ 34.5 g	Niacin:............. 3.55 mg
Phosphate:.......... 746 mg	Calcium:............ 494 mg
Potassium:.......... 320 mg	Iron:................ 7.3 mg
Zinc:.............. 4.05 mg	Cholesterol:........ 799 mg
Vitamin A:......... 1300 iu	Sodium:........... 1293 mg

Eggs with Shrimp Sauce

2   tablespoons butter
2   tablespoons flour
10   ounce can cream of shrimp soup
1   soup can milk
½   cup cheddar cheese, grated

Melt butter in saucepan and stir in flour. Add soup and milk, cook until thickened. Add cheese and cook until cheese is melted. Pour over soft scrambled eggs. Makes 2 servings.

Nutritional Analysis Per Serving:

Calories:	546.5	Vitamin C:	0 mg
Protein:	19.5 g	Thiamine:	.15 mg
Carbohydrates:	25.5 g	Riboflavin:	.5 mg
Fat:	41.5 g	Niacin:	1.05 mg
Phosphate:	364.5 mg	Calcium:	444 mg
Potassium:	335.5 mg	Iron:	1.05 mg
Zinc:	4 mg	Cholesterol:	112 mg
Vitamin A:	1094.5 iu	Sodium:	1687.5 mg

Onion, Cheese and Egg Bake

4   onions, finely chopped
1   green pepper, finely chopped
10 ounces cheddar cheese, grated
6   eggs
6   tablespoons milk
2   tablespoons worcestershire sauce
    salt and pepper

Cook the onion in lightly salted boiling water for 5 minutes. Drain, place half in ovenproof dish. Sprinkle with half the chopped pepper, then half the cheese. Repeat layers. Beat remaining ingredients together, with salt and pepper to taste. Pour into the dish and cook in oven at 350 degrees for 30 minutes. Makes 6 servings.

Nutritional Analysis Per Serving:

Calories:	228.17	Vitamin C:	46.5 mg
Protein:	14 g	Thiamine:	.12 mg
Carbohydrates:	13.67 g	Riboflavin:	.33 mg
Fat:	13.5 g	Niacin:	.45 mg
Phosphate:	265.17 mg	Calcium:	250.83 mg
Potassium:	380.5 mg	Iron:	2.18 mg
Zinc:	1.8 mg	Cholesterol:	273.33 mg
Vitamin A:	679.33 iu	Sodium:	279.5 mg

Egg and Sausage Casserole

1   pound sausage
12   eggs
1   can cream of mushroom soup
½   cup milk
¼   pound cheddar cheese, grated

Brown sausage in skillet, stirring until crumbly; drain and remove. Scramble eggs in a small amount of pan drippings until partially set. Mix soup and milk in bowl. Layer sausage and eggs in a 1½ quart casserole. Top with soup mixture and cheese. Bake at 350 degrees until cheese melts. Makes 6 servings.

Nutritional Analysis Per Serving:

Calories:.........641.17		Vitamin C: ....17 mg	
Protein: ....30.67 g		Thiamine:............7 mg	
Carbohydrates: ....6.5 g		Riboflavin: ....68 mg	
Fat: ....54 g		Niacin: ....3.2 mg	
Phosphate: ....418.5 mg		Calcium:...........231.5 mg	
Potassium:........408.17 mg		Iron: ....4.03 mg	
Zinc: ....4.6 mg		Cholesterol: ....586 mg	
Vitamin A: ....721.33 iu		Sodium: ....1363.33 mg	

Broccoli Beef

½   pound twice ground beef
3   cups cooked broccoli, finely chopped
½   cup evaporated milk
1   egg, slightly beaten
1   can cream of chicken soup
1   cup cheddar cheese, grated
1   cup bread stuffing mix
3   tablespoons butter

Place ground beef in skillet and stir until brown; drain. Add broccoli, milk, egg and cream of chicken soup; mix well. Place beef mixture in lightly buttered casserole. Combine cheese, stuffing mix and butter and sprinkle over beef mixture. Bake at 350 degrees for 25 minutes. (Note): May substitute asparagus, cauliflower, eggplant or zucchini for broccoli. Makes 4 servings.

Nutritional Analysis Per Serving:

Calories:	503.5	Vitamin C:	105.25 mg
Protein:	29.25 g	Thiamine:	.23 mg
Carbohydrates:	20.75 g	Riboflavin:	.63 mg
Fat:	34.75 g	Niacin:	4.18 mg
Phosphate:	445 mg	Calcium:	431 mg
Potassium:	651 mg	Iron:	3.58 mg
Zinc:	4.28 mg	Cholesterol:	192.25 mg
Vitamin A:	4072 iu	Sodium:	1133.5 mg

Skillet Sausage

1   onion, cut into pieces
½   green pepper, cut into pieces
1   pound pork sausage, twice ground
1   16 ounce can tomatoes, undrained
       and cut up fine
½   cup tomato juice
1   teaspoon salt
½   teaspoon chili powder
1   cup dairy sour cream

Place onion and green pepper in blender and blend until finely chopped. Cook sausage, onion and pepper until the meat browns; break up sausage as it cooks. Drain off fat. Add remaining ingredients, except sour cream. Cover and simmer for 20 minutes. Add sour cream but do not boil. Makes 6 servings.

Nutritional Analysis Per Serving:

Calories:.........452.83	Vitamin C:............36 mg
Protein: ....15.83 g	Thiamine: ....66 mg
Carbohydrates: ....7.5 g	Riboflavin:...........35 mg
Fat: ....40 g	Niacin: ....3.61 mg
Phosphate: ....175.66 mg	Calcium:...........76.83 mg
Potassium:........517.83 mg	Iron: ....2.56 mg
Zinc: ....2.71 mg	Cholesterol:.........80.5 mg
Vitamin A: ....1197.83 iu	Sodium: ....1267.5 mg

One Dish Pancake

1	cup all-purpose flour
1	tablespoon baking powder
1	egg, beaten
¾	cup milk
1	cup sharp American cheese, shredded
3	tablespoons bacon drippings

Combine flour and baking powder. Combine egg, milk and bacon drippings. Pour into greased and floured 10x15 inch baking pan and spread evenly. Bake at 425 degrees for 15 minutes. Remove from oven and sprinkle with cheese. Bake for another 5 minutes or until cheese melts. Makes 2 servings.

Nutritional Analysis Per Serving:

Calories:	683	Vitamin C:	1 mg
Protein:	25 g	Thiamine:	.50 mg
Carbohydrates:	53 g	Riboflavin:	.65 mg
Fat:	40.5 g	Niacin:	3.5 mg
Phosphate:	609.5 mg	Calcium:	515 mg
Potassium:	320.5 mg	Iron:	2.60 mg
Zinc:	2.95 mg	Cholesterol:	204 mg
Vitamin A:	916 iu	Sodium:	1031.5 mg

Layered Casserole Italiano

5	cups zucchini, finely diced
1	cup onion, minced
1	small garlic clove, crushed
2	tablespoons butter
1	pound twice ground beef
1	cup minute rice
1	teaspoon basil
16	ounce carton cream-style cottage cheese
1	can tomato soup
1	cup sharp American cheese, shredded

Cook zucchini in a small amount of salted water until tender; drain. In a skillet, saute onion and garlic in butter. When onions are golden add ground beef and stir until brown. Stir in the rice and basil. Arrange ½ the zucchini in the bottom of 2½ quart casserole and layer the ground beef mixture and remaining zucchini over top. Mix soups with ⅔ cup water and pour over the top, sprinkle cheese on top. Bake at 350 degrees for 40 minutes or until lightly brown. Makes 8 servings.

Nutritional Analysis Per Serving:

Calories:	300.13	Vitamin C:	23.88 mg
Protein:	23.88 g	Thiamine:	.15 mg
Carbohydrates:	16.75 g	Riboflavin:	.34 mg
Fat:	15.38 g	Niacin:	4.06 mg
Phosphate:	321.38 mg	Calcium:	159.25 mg
Potassium:	469.5 mg	Iron:	2.43 mg
Zinc:	3.18 mg	Cholesterol:	69 mg
Vitamin A:	1030.75 iu	Sodium:	786.25 mg

Spinach Quiche

2   10 ounce packages frozen chopped spinach
1   pie crust
1   pound provolone cheese, shredded
3   eggs, beaten
½   cup sour cream

Cook spinach and drain. Cover pie crust with shredded cheese. Combine spinach, eggs and sour cream. Spoon onto cheese. Bake at 325 degrees for 45 minutes. Makes 6 servings.

Nutritional Analysis Per Serving:

Calories:	381	Vitamin C:	16.33 mg
Protein:	18.33 g	Thiamine:	.18 mg
Carbohydrates:	18.5 g	Riboflavin:	.41 mg
Fat:	26.5 g	Niacin:	1.25 mg
Phosphate:	334.5 mg	Calcium:	493.83 mg
Potassium:	393.5 mg	Iron:	2.87 mg
Zinc:	2.5 mg	Cholesterol:	164.83 mg
Vitamin A:	7309.5 iu	Sodium:	365.17 mg

Spinach Hot Dish

1½	pounds twice ground beef
1	small onion, minced
2	10 ounce packages frozen spinach, cooked and finely chopped
½	teaspoon garlic powder
¼	teaspoon oregano
6	eggs
¼	cup milk

Mix ground beef and onion in skillet and stir until lightly browned. Mix in spinach and seasonings. In a bowl mix eggs and milk together and beat until light. Add to the spinach mixture, mixing well. Cook over low heat until the eggs are cooked, stirring occasionally. Makes 4 servings.

Nutritional Analysis Per Serving:

Calories:.........432.75	Vitamin C: ....26.5 mg
Protein: ....47.75 g	Thiamine:............ .3 mg
Carbohydrates:.........8 g	Riboflavin: .... .73 mg
Fat: ....23 g	Niacin: ....8.3 mg
Phosphate: ....493 mg	Calcium:..........221.75 mg
Potassium:........962.25 mg	Iron: ....8.7 mg
Zinc: ....8.5 mg	Cholesterol:.......491.75 mg
Vitamin A:.........10526 iu	Sodium: ....254.75 mg

92

Fancy Cabbage Rolls

1   small head cabbage, finely chopped
1   pound twice ground beef
½   cup onion, minced
½   cup rice
½   teaspoon salt
¼   teaspoon pepper
1   can tomato soup
½   cup cheese, grated

Place cabbage over the bottom of a 9x13 inch baking dish. In a skillet, combine ground beef and onion and stir until brown. Stir in rice, salt and pepper and mix well. Spoon beef mixture over cabbage. In a saucepan mix soup with 1½ cups water and bring to a boil. Pour over beef mixture, top with cheese. Bake at 350 degrees for 1½ hours. Stir lightly before serving. For a more spicy flavor, use 1 can of tomato sauce in place of tomato soup. Makes 4 servings.

Nutritional Analysis Per Serving:

Calories:..........425.5	Vitamin C:...........66 mg
Protein: ....31.75 g	Thiamine:............3 mg
Carbohydrates:........38 g	Riboflavin:...........38 mg
Fat:...............16.25 g	Niacin: ....7.25 mg
Phosphate: ....353.25 mg	Calcium..........209.25 mg
Potassium:........750.75 mg	Iron: ....4.83 mg
Zinc:.................6 mg	Cholesterol:.........94.5 mg
Vitamin A: ....1023.75 iu	Sodium: ....1068.75 mg

Baked Chile

1	tablespoon salad oil
1	pound lean beef, twice ground
½	cup celery, finely chopped
1	onion, finely chopped
1	can condensed tomato soup
¾	cup water
1	tablespoon paprika
2	teaspoons chili powder
1/8	teaspoon garlic powder
1/8	teaspoon ground allspice
½	cup shredded sharp cheddar cheese

In a medium-sized frying pan, heat the oil over medium heat and crumble in the ground beef. Brown meat. Add the celery and onion; saute until onion is soft. Blend in the tomato soup, water, paprika, chili powder, garlic powder, and allspice. Pour into an ungreased 1½ quart casserole. Cover and bake at 350 degrees for 45 minutes. Uncover, skim off fat, sprinkle cheese over top, and return to oven until cheese melts. Makes 4 servings.

Nutritional Analysis Per Serving:

Calories:	339	Vitamin C:	11 mg
Protein:	28.5 g	Thiamine:	13 mg
Carbohydrates:	12.25 g	Riboflavin:	3 mg
Fat:	19.25 g	Niacin:	5.98 mg
Phosphate:	301.75 mg	Calcium:	134.5 mg
Potassium:	510 mg	Iron:	3.7 mg
Zinc:	5.05 mg	Cholesterol:	94.5 mg
Vitamin A:	849.25 iu	Sodium:	776.25 mg

Country Pie

1   pound twice ground beef
½   cup bread crumbs
1/8   teaspoon pepper
1½   teaspoons salt
2½   cups tomato sauce
1⅓   cups rice
1   cup grated cheese

Combine ground beef, bread crumbs, pepper, with 1 teaspoon salt and 1 cup tomato sauce in bowl, mixing well. Press mixture into 9 inch pie plate. Combine rice, cheese, ½ teaspoon salt, 1 cup water and remaining 1½ cups tomato sauce in bowl, mixing well. Pour into prepared pie plate. Cover and bake at 350 degrees for 25 minutes. Sprinkle additional cheese over top and bake an additional 10 minutes, uncovered, or until cheese melts. Makes 4 servings.

Nutritional Analysis Per Serving:

Calories:	629.75	Vitamin C:	2076 mg
Protein:	38 g	Thiamine:	.48 mg
Carbohydrates:	71 g	Riboflavin:	.43 mg
Fat:	20 g	Niacin:	9.5 mg
Phosphate:	524.25 mg	Calcium:	270 mg
Potassium:	471.5 mg	Iron:	6.23 mg
Zinc:	6.33 mg	Cholesterol:	110 mg
Vitamin A:	2076 iu	Sodium:	2107.75 mg

Hot Tamale Pie Casserole

1½   pounds twice ground beef
2   large onions, finely chopped
16   ounce can tomato sauce
3   tablespoons chili powder
¾   cup cornmeal
     salt to taste
     pepper to taste

Place ground beef in skillet and stir until brown; drain. Add onion, tomato sauce, and chili powder and cook until thick. Mix cornmeal with enough cold water in bowl to make paste. In a saucepan place 1½ cups of water and bring to a boil. Add cornmeal mixture and 1 teaspoon salt to boiling water, stirring constantly and cook until thick. Pour cornmeal mixture into 2 quart casserole and top with ground beef mixture. Bake at 375 degrees for 20 minutes. Makes 6 servings.

Nutritional Analysis Per Serving:

Calories:.........293.17	Vitamin C: ....29.17 mg
Protein: ....26.33 g	Thiamine:..............2 mg
Carbohydrates:........23 g	Riboflavin:............28 mg
Fat: ....10 g	Niacin: ....6.63 mg
Phosphate: ....282.67 mg	Calcium:...........31.83 mg
Potassium:........394.67 mg	Iron: ....4.38 mg
Zinc: ....4.77 mg	Cholesterol:........79.83 mg
Vitamin A: ....1046.83 iu	Sodium:.............547 mg

Beef Delight

2	pounds twice ground beef
6	cups bread crumbs
1	large onion, finely chopped
¼	pound margarine, melted
2	cans cream of chicken soup
2	cans cream of celery soup
	salt and pepper to taste
	sage and oregano to taste

Press ground beef over bottom of 9x13 inch lightly greased baking dish. Combine bread crumbs, onion, margarine, salt and pepper in bowl, mixing well. Pour bread crumb mixture over ground beef. Mix soup in bowl and pour over bread crumb mixture, lightly sprinkle with sage and oregano. Bake at 350 degrees for 1½ hours or until brown. Makes 8 servings.

Nutritional Analysis Per Serving:

Calories:	483	Vitamin C:	1.63 mg
Protein:	29 g	Thiamine:	.14 mg
Carbohydrates:	26.25 g	Riboflavin:	.29 mg
Fat:	28.75 g	Niacin:	5.74 mg
Phosphate:	275.25 mg	Calcium:	87.38 mg
Potassium:	438.38 mg	Iron:	3.85 mg
Zinc:	5.11 mg	Cholesterol:	91.13 mg
Vitamin A:	869.5 iu	Sodium:	1538.5 mg

Spaghetti Casserole

1	pound twice ground beef
1	onion, finely chopped
½	green pepper, finely chopped
1	can tomato soup
1	can cream of mushroom soup
1½	cups grated cheese
½	pound spaghetti, cooked, drained and finely chopped
	salt and pepper to taste

In a skillet brown ground beef with onion and green pepper, stirring until brown. Stir in soups and 1 cup water and simmer for several minutes. Add spaghetti, 1 cup cheese, salt and pepper, mixing well. Place mixture into 2½ quart casserole and sprinkle remaining ½ cup of cheese on top. Bake in moderate oven until cheese is bubbly and melted. About 20 minutes. Makes 4 servings.

Nutritional Analysis Per Serving:

Calories:. 673.5		Vitamin C: . . . . 36 mg	
Protein: . . . . 42.25 g		Thiamine: . . . . .38 mg	
Carbohydrates: . . . . . 53.75 g		Riboflavin: . . . . .6 mg	
Fat: . . . . 31.75 g		Niacin: . . . . 8.15 mg	
Phosphate: . . . . 551.75 mg		Calcium: . . . . 369.75 mg	
Potassium: . . . . 675.5 mg		Iron: . . . . 5.63 mg	
Zinc: . . . . 7 mg		Cholesterol: . . . . 130.25 mg	
Vitamin A: . . . . 1233 iu		Sodium: . . . . 1529.75 mg	

Colorado Hash

3   large onions, finely chopped
1   large green pepper, finely chopped
3   tablespoons cooking oil
1   pound twice ground beef
16   ounce can tomato sauce
½   cup rice
1   teaspoon chili powder
1/8 teaspoon pepper

In a large skillet, saute onions and green pepper in oil until onions are golden. Add ground beef and stir until brown. Add remaining ingredients and mix well. Place into 2 quart baking dish and bake covered, at 350 degrees for 45 minutes, remove cover and bake an additional 15 minutes. Makes 8 servings.

Nutritional Analysis Per Serving:

Calories:	225.13	Vitamin C:	49.75 mg
Protein:	14.13 g	Thiamine:	.15 mg
Carbohydrates:	18.75 g	Riboflavin:	.16 mg
Fat:	10.25 g	Niacin:	3.79 mg
Phosphate:	172.38 mg	Calcium:	33.25 mg
Potassium:	294.5 mg	Iron:	2.5 mg
Zinc:	2.58 mg	Cholesterol:	39.88 mg
Vitamin A:	815.5 iu	Sodium:	497.63 mg

Lamb Loaves

1 pound lean lamb, twice ground
½ pound lean beef, twice ground
2 cups soft french bread crumbs
1 can condensed onion soup
¼ teaspoon oregano
   mint leaves

Mix ground lamb, beef, crumbs, soup, and oregano, stirring until blended. Spoon meat mixture into 12 ungreased 2½ inch muffin cups, pressing in lightly. Bake, uncovered, in a 400 degree oven for 15 minutes. Garnish with fresh mint leaves. Makes 4 servings.

Nutritional Analysis Per Serving:

Calories:	716	Vitamin C:	0 mg
Protein:	45.75 g	Thiamine:	45 mg
Carbohydrates:	42 g	Riboflavin:	55 mg
Fat:	38.75 g	Niacin:	10.18 mg
Phosphate:	367.25 mg	Calcium:	66.75 mg
Potassium:	584 mg	Iron:	4.68 mg
Zinc:	3 mg	Cholesterol:	168 mg
Vitamin A:	8.5 iu	Sodium:	1603.25 mg

Orange Lamb Patties

1½   pounds lean lamb, twice ground
¼   cup fine bread crumbs
1   egg
1½   teaspoons ground coriander
½   teaspoon grated orange peel
¼   cup orange juice
2   tablespoons soy sauce

Mix together the lamb, crumbs, egg, coriander, orange peel, orange juice, and soy. Make six patties. Place in broiler pan about four inches from heat and broil for 5 minutes on each side. Makes 6 servings.

Nutritional Analysis Per Serving:

Calories: 321	Vitamin C: . . . . 5.17 mg
Protein: . . . . 20.17 g	Thiamine: . . . . .13 mg
Carbohydrates: . . . . . . 4.67 g	Riboflavin: . . . . .25 mg
Fat: . . . . 24 g	Niacin: . . . . 4.27 mg
Phosphate: . . . . 172.5 mg	Calcium: . . . . 25.33 mg
Potassium: . . . . 303.33 mg	Iron: . . . . 1.63 mg
Zinc: . . . . .15 mg	Cholesterol: . . . . 124.5 mg
Vitamin A: . . . . 59.83 iu	Sodium: . . . . 863.5 mg

Mexican Casserole

1   pound twice ground beef
21   ounce can hot chili without beans
8   ounce mozzarella cheese, shredded
1   package tortilla chips, crushed fine

Brown ground beef in skillet, stirring until brown. Layer ground beef, chili, half the cheese in a casserole. Top with remaining cheese and tortilla chips. Bake at 375 degrees for 30 minutes or until heated through. Makes 4 servings.

Nutritional Analysis Per Serving:

Calories:	953.75	Vitamin C:	0 mg
Protein:	59.5 g	Thiamine:	.18 mg
Carbohydrates:	35.5 g	Riboflavin:	.63 mg
Fat:	62.25 g	Niacin:	9.35 mg
Phosphate:	850.75 mg	Calcium:	672.75 mg
Potassium:	820 mg	Iron:	6.55 mg
Zinc:	10.03 mg	Cholesterol:	187.75 mg
Vitamin A:	860 iu	Sodium:	1472.5 mg

Baked Chilies Rellenos

First layer

1	pound beef, twice ground
½	cup onion, finely chopped
½	teaspoon salt
¼	teaspoon black pepper
1	4 ounce can green chilies, finely chopped
1½	cups sharp cheddar cheese, shredded

Brown ground beef and chopped onion in skillet. Drain. Sprinkle meat with ½ teaspoon salt and ¼ teaspoon pepper. Empty one 4 ounce can of chopped green chilies in 10x6x1½ inch baking dish; sprinkle with cheese and top with meat.

Second layer

1	4 ounce can green chilies, finely chopped
4	eggs, beaten
1½	cups milk
¼	cup flour
½	teaspoon salt
4	dashes hot pepper sauce
1	dash black pepper

Arrange one 4 ounce can green chilies over meat. Combine 4 beaten eggs, 1½ cups milk, ¼ cup flour, ½ teaspoon salt, hot pepper sauce and dash of black pepper; beat until smooth. Pour over chili mixture. Bake in oven at 350 degrees for 45 minutes. Cut into squares to serve. Makes 6 servings.

Nutritional Analysis Per Serving (continued on page 104)

Nutritional Analysis Per Serving:

Calories: 359	Vitamin C: . . . . 24 mg
Protein: . . . . 29.66 g	Thiamine: . . . . .13 mg
Carbohydrates: . . . . . 10.17 g	Riboflavin: . . . . .45 mg
Fat: . . . . 21.67 g	Niacin: . . . . 3.8 mg
Phosphate: . . . . 407.33 mg	Calcium: . . . . 311.5 mg
Potassium: . . . . 505 mg	Iron: . . . . 3.2 mg
Zinc: . . . . 4.65 mg	Cholesterol: . . . . 277.67 mg
Vitamin A: . . . . 722.33 iu	Sodium: . . . . 685.5 mg

Cashew Butter

2   cups cashews
2   tablespoons butter
½   teaspoon salt

Place cashews in food processor or blender. Process until cashews are very finely ground. Add butter and salt and continue processing until smooth. Makes 1 cup or 16 servings.

Nutritional Analysis Per Serving:

Calories: 169.62	Vitamin C: . . . . 0 mg
Protein: . . . . 4.81 g	Thiamine: . . . . .12 mg
Carbohydrates: . . . . . . 8.19 g	Riboflavin: . . . . .07 mg
Fat: . . . . 14.19 g	Niacin: . . . . .51 mg
Phosphate: . . . . 104.93 mg	Calcium: . . . . 11.5 mg
Potassium: . . . . 130.38 mg	Iron: . . . . 1.07 mg
Zinc: . . . . 1.23 mg	Cholesterol: . . . . 3.81 mg
Vitamin A: . . . . 81.5 iu	Sodium: . . . . 91.3 mg

Potato Pie

2   cups potatoes, cooked and mashed
1   pound cottage cheese
½   cup sour cream
2   eggs
1/8 teaspoon pepper
3   tablespoons parmesan cheese

Put cottage cheese in a blender container and blend until smooth. Mix cottage cheese with all other ingredients and into baking dish. Bake in a covered dish at 400 degrees for 50 minutes. Makes 6 servings.

Nutritional Analysis Per Serving:

Calories: 170	Vitamin C: . . . . 7.17 mg
Protein: . . . . 13.17 g	Thiamine: . . . . .08 mg
Carbohydrates: . . . . . 12.17 g	Riboflavin: . . . . .23 mg
Fat: . . . . 7.5 g	Niacin: . . . . .80 mg
Phosphate: . . . . 187.83 mg	Calcium: . . . . 125 mg
Potassium: . . . . 286.17 mg	Iron: . . . . .77 mg
Zinc: . . . . .8 mg	Cholesterol: . . . . .97.33 mg
Vitamin A: . . . . 278.33 iu	Sodium: . . . . 661.83 mg

Meat Dressing

½   pound chicken livers
1   pound beef, twice ground
1   pound pork, twice ground
1   cup bell pepper, finely chopped
1   cup celery, finely chopped
1   teaspoon salt
½   teaspoon pepper
1   bunch green onions, finely chopped
1   bunch parsley, finely chopped

Place chicken livers in large pot of boiling water and cook until tender. Drain and reserve stock. Chop livers in blender container until finely chopped. In a skillet brown beef and pork, when brown, add the celery and bell pepper. Cook over low heat until tender. Add salt and pepper. Stir in stock and enough water to make 3½ cups liquid. Add onions, meat and parsley. Simmer for 45 minutes, stirring occasionally. Serves 8.

Nutritional Analysis Per Serving:

Calories:	276.25	Vitamin C:	32.13 mg
Protein:	33.88 g	Thiamine:	.45 mg
Carbohydrates:	2.38 g	Riboflavin:	.75 mg
Fat:	13.75 g	Niacin:	6.68 mg
Phosphate:	313.13 mg	Calcium:	35.13 mg
Potassium:	434.25 mg	Iron:	6.26 mg
Zinc:	5.06 mg	Cholesterol:	264.13 mg
Vitamin A:	5286.5 iu	Sodium:	871.88 mg

Mushroom Shrimp

2   slices of onion, finely chopped
1   small potato, grated
3   tablespoons butter
1   tablespoon chives, finely chopped
1   10¾ ounce can cream of mushroom soup
5   large shrimp, finely chopped

In a sauce pan melt the butter. Add the onion, potato and chives. Cook on low heat until onions are clear. Add cream of mushroom soup and milk. Simmer for 5 minutes. Add shrimp and simmer for additional 3 minutes. Serve hot. Makes 2 servings.

Nutritional Analysis Per Serving:

Calories:	462	Vitamin C:	12.5 mg
Protein:	41.5 g	Thiamine:	.10 mg
Carbohydrates:	19.5 g	Riboflavin:	.15 mg
Fat:	23.5 g	Niacin:	8 mg
Phosphate:	418 mg	Calcium:	169 mg
Potassium:	742 mg	Iron:	4.1 mg
Zinc:	3.75 mg	Cholesterol:	369.5 mg
Vitamin A:	688 iu	Sodium:	951.5 mg

Cheesy-Potato Bake

4   large potatoes, peeled and thinly sliced
2   cups shredded mozzarella cheese
2   ounce package white sauce mix
1½   cups milk
¼   teaspoon pepper
      paprika

Alternate layers of potatoes and cheese in 2 quart buttered baking dish. Prepare white sauce mix according to package directions, using 1½ cups milk. Add pepper. Pour over potatoes; sprinkle with paprika. Bake at 350 degrees for 1 hour. Makes 6 servings.

Nutritional Analysis Per Serving:

Calories:	315	Vitamin C:	15.5 mg
Protein:	14.66 g	Thiamine:	.13 mg
Carbohydrates:	20.16 g	Riboflavin:	.33 mg
Fat:	19.83 g	Niacin:	1.3 mg
Phosphate:	328 mg	Calcium:	405.33 mg
Potassium:	444.5 mg	Iron:	.87 mg
Zinc:	1.83 mg	Cholesterol:	65.17 mg
Vitamin A:	667.67 iu	Sodium:	617.33 mg

Party Potatoes

10   potatoes
8   ounce package cream cheese, softened
8   ounce package sour cream
      garlic salt to taste

Cook potatoes; mash. Blend cream cheese and sour cream. Add to potatoes and mix well. Place in greased casserole and bake at 350 degrees for 25 minutes. Makes 8 servings.

Nutritional Analysis Per Serving:

Calories:	262.25	Vitamin C:	27.25 mg
Protein:	6.13 g	Thiamine:	.16 mg
Carbohydrates:	26.25 g	Riboflavin:	.15 mg
Fat:	15.38 g	Niacin:	2.08 mg
Phosphate:	121.38 mg	Calcium:	61.13 mg
Potassium:	550 mg	Iron:	1.21 mg
Zinc:	.73 mg	Cholesterol:	42.38 mg
Vitamin A:	603.38 iu	Sodium:	101.88 mg

German Potatoes

6   large potatoes, shredded
½   cup onion, finely chopped
2   eggs, beaten
½   cup milk
1   teaspoon salt
¼   teaspoon pepper
5   slices of bacon, finely diced

Mix all ingredients and pour into greased 9x12 inch baking dish. Bake covered at 375 degrees for 1 hour. Serves 6.

Nutritional Analysis Per Serving *(continued on page 111)*

GERMAN POTATOES (continued from page 110)

Nutritional Analysis Per Serving:

Calories:	193	Vitamin C:	25.33 mg
Protein:	7.67 g	Thiamine:	0.2 mg
Carbohydrates:	28.17 g	Riboflavin:	0.17 mg
Fat:	5.67 g	Niacin:	2.67 mg
Phosphate:	146.17 mg	Calcium:	51.17 mg
Potassium:	695.5 mg	Iron:	1.52 mg
Zinc:	0.9 mg	Cholesterol:	89.67 mg
Vitamin A:	126.5 iu	Sodium:	492.17 mg

Potato Casserole

6	Potatoes, peeled
	salt
1	cup sour cream
1	can cream of chicken soup
¼	teaspoon pepper
¼	teaspoon curry powder
4	hard-boiled eggs, finely diced
½	cup soft bread crumbs
½	cup sharp cheddar cheese, shredded

Cook potatoes in boiling salted water in saucepan until tender. Cut into fine cubes. Mix sour cream, soup, 1 teaspoon salt, pepper, curry powder in bowl. Layer the potatoes, egg and soup mixture in casserole. Mix bread crumbs and cheese and sprinkle over casserole. Bake at 350 degrees for 30 minutes. Makes 6 servings.

Nutritional Analysis Per Serving:

Calories:	313.83	Vitamin C:	30.33 mg
Protein:	11.5 g	Thiamine:	.22 mg
Carbohydrates:	32.33 g	Riboflavin:	.25 mg
Fat:	15.67 g	Niacin:	2.62 mg
Phosphate:	224.33 mg	Calcium:	1444.83 mg
Potassium:	739.83 mg	Iron:	1.9 mg
Zinc:	1.53 mg	Cholesterol:	187.83 mg
Vitamin A:	674.33 iu	Sodium:	585.67 mg

Baked Hash Browns

2   pounds frozen hashed brown potatoes
2   cups cheddar cheese, grated
½   cup onion, finely chopped
¼   teaspoon pepper
1   cup butter, melted
1   can cream of chicken soup
1   cup corn flakes, crushed

Combine potatoes, cheese, onion, pepper, ½ cup butter and chicken soup. Place in 2 quart casserole. Combine ½ cup butter and corn flakes. Sprinkle over potato mixture. Bake at 350 degrees for 1 hour. Makes 6 servings.

Nutritional Analysis Per Serving:

Calories:	440.33	Vitamin C:	12.33 mg
Protein:	14.17 g	Thiamine:	.17 mg
Carbohydrates:	37.5 g	Riboflavin:	.28 mg
Fat:	26.67 g	Niacin:	3.1 mg
Phosphate:	294.17 mg	Calcium:	300.17 mg
Potassium:	569.33 mg	Iron:	1.7 mg
Zinc:	3.67 mg	Cholesterol:	43.5 mg
Vitamin A:	759.17 iu	Sodium:	1050.33 mg

Hashed Brown Casserole

1	16 ounce package frozen hashed brown potatoes
1	can cream of celery soup
1	can cream of mushroom soup
½	cup onion, minced
½	cup green pepper, minced
	paprika
	parsley, finely chopped

Combine first 5 ingredients in bowl, mixing well. Spoon into greased 9x13 baking dish. Top with paprika and parsley. Bake at 350 degrees for 1½ hours. Makes 8 servings.

Nutritional Analysis Per Serving:

Calories:	160	Vitamin C:	12.37 mg
Protein:	2.63 g	Thiamine:	.05 mg
Carbohydrates:	18 g	Riboflavin:	.08 mg
Fat:	9 g	Niacin:	1.08 mg
Phosphate:	61.5 mg	Calcium:	36 mg
Potassium:	269 mg	Iron:	.73 mg
Zinc:	.39 mg	Cholesterol:	5.25 mg
Vitamin A:	123.125 iu	Sodium:	706.63 mg

Sweet Potato Puree

2   sweet potatoes
1½   tablespoons butter
1½   tablespoons heavy cream
1   tablespoon orange juice
        peel of ½ orange

Peel and cut sweet potatoes into 1 inch cubes. Boil until tender, about 15 minutes. Place sweet potatoes and the rest of ingredients in a food processor or blender. Blend until smooth, adding extra cream if necessary. Makes 2 servings.

Nutritional Analysis Per Serving:

Calories:	276.5	Vitamin C:	29 mg
Protein:	3 g	Thiamine:	.1 mg
Carbohydrates:	38 g	Riboflavin:	.1 mg
Fat:	13.5 g	Niacin:	.8 mg
Phosphate:	75.5 mg	Calcium:	59 mg
Potassium:	357.5 mg	Iron:	1.05 mg
Zinc:	.4 mg	Cholesterol:	38 mg
Vitamin A:	972.15 iu	Sodium:	374 mg

Steamed Sweet Potatoes and Parsnips

      water
¼   cup butter or margarine
1½   pounds sweet potatoes, peeled and cut in
         julienne strips
1   pound parsnips, peeled and cut in
         julienne strips
      pinch of nutmeg

In a large skillet bring about ½ inch water to a simmer. Add butter and heat until butter melts. Add sweet potatoes and parsnips. Cover and cook over medium-high heat 2 minutes. Remove cover; cook about 2 minutes longer until tender. Sprinkle with nutmeg before serving. Makes 6 servings.

Nutritional Analysis Per Serving:

Calories:	221.67	Vitamin C:	23 mg
Protein:	2.67 g	Thiamine:	13 mg
Carbohydrates:	35.33 g	Riboflavin:	1 mg
Fat:	8.33 g	Niacin:	68 mg
Phosphate:	84.16 mg	Calcium:	59.5 mg
Potassium:	457.67 mg	Iron:	1.07 mg
Zinc:	55 mg	Cholesterol:	20.67 mg
Vitamin A:	8534.33 iu	Sodium:	92.83 mg

Southern Sweet Potatoes

2   16 ounce cans sweet potatoes
¾   cup honey
2   eggs, beaten
¼   cup butter, melted
⅓   cup butter, melted
⅓   cup flour
⅓   cup milk

Mix sweet potatoes and eggs with ¼ cup butter. Pour into 9x13 inch casserole. Combine honey, flour, milk and ⅓ cup butter, mixing well. Pour over sweet potatoes. Bake at 350 degrees for 30 minutes. Makes 6 servings.

Nutritional Analysis Per Serving:

Calories:	547	Vitamin C:	13.33 mg
Protein:	5 g	Thiamine:	0.12 mg
Carbohydrates:	85 g	Riboflavin:	0.17 mg
Fat:	22.83 g	Niacin:	1.48 mg
Phosphate:	100.17 mg	Calcium:	54.3 mg
Potassium:	266.5 mg	Iron:	1.92 mg
Zinc:	0.62 mg	Cholesterol:	138.67 mg
Vitamin A:	8858.5 iu	Sodium:	312.83 mg

Sweet Potato and Apple Casserole

5   cups sweet potatoes, cooked and mashed
3   cups applesauce (unsweetened)
½   cup honey
2   tablespoons orange juice
2   tablespoons margarine

Layer sweet potatoes and apple sauce in greased casserole. Combine juice, honey, with ½ cup water and pour over layers. Dot with margarine. Bake at 350 degrees for 30 minutes. Makes 8 servings.

Nutritional Analysis Per Serving:

Calories:	307	Vitamin C:	27.75 mg
Protein:	2.87 g	Thiamine:	16 mg
Carbohydrates:	68.5 g	Riboflavin:	11 mg
Fat:	3.87 g	Niacin:	1 mg
Phosphate:	80.25 mg	Calcium:	56.75 mg
Potassium:	463.37 mg	Iron:	1.66 mg
Zinc:	58 mg	Cholesterol:	0 mg
Vitamin A:	12504.25 iu	Sodium:	78 mg

Egg and Asparagus Casserole

4	slices white bread, trimmed and cubed
6	tablespoons butter, melted
2	tablespoons flour
1½	cups milk
1	tablespoon parsley, finely chopped
¼	teaspoon pepper
¾	teaspoon salt
½	cup American cheese, grated
12	ounces asparagus tips, cooked, drained and chopped fine
4	hard-boiled eggs, chopped fine
½	cup bread crumbs

Toss bread cubes with 2 tablespoons butter in bowl. Mix flour with 4 tablespoons butter in saucepan. Stir constantly, until thick. Add milk gradually until smooth. Add parsley, pepper, salt and American cheese. Place ½ bread cubes in greased baking dish. Layer asparagus and eggs over bread cubes. Pour cheese sauce over all ingredients. Sprinkle top with bread crumbs. Bake at 350 for 15 minutes. Makes 4 servings.

Nutritional Analysis Per Serving:

Calories:	466.25	Vitamin C:	11,25 mg
Protein:	17 g	Thiamine:	.3 mg
Carbohydrates:	31 g	Riboflavin:	.48 mg
Fat:	30.75 g	Niacin:	2.15 mg
Phosphate:	344 mg	Calcium:	275.75 mg
Potassium:	362.75 mg	Iron:	2.8 mg
Zinc:	2 mg	Cholesterol:	313.25 mg
Vitamin A:	1560.5 iu	Sodium:	1201.5 mg

Favorite Broccoli Casserole

10   ounce package chopped broccoli
8   ounce jar Cheese Whiz
1   can cream of mushroom soup
1   cup cooked rice
½   cup onion, minced
4   tablespoons butter

Combine all ingredients in 2 quart buttered casserole. Bake at 350 degrees for 25 minutes. Makes 6 servings.

Nutritional Analysis Per Serving:

Calories:..........279.17		Vitamin C: 23.33	mg
Protein: 9.17	g	Thiamine:........... .08	mg
Carbohydrates: 17.67	g	Riboflavin: .... .27	mg
Fat: 19.67	g	Niacin: .... .87	mg
Phosphate: 324	mg	Calcium:..........256.67	mg
Potassium: 246	mg	Iron: .... .93	mg
Zinc: 1.48	mg	Cholesterol:........44.83	mg
Vitamin A: 1617.33	iu	Sodium: 984.5	mg

Party Broccoli Casserole

3   10 ounce packages frozen chopped broccoli,
      cooked and drained
1   2 ounce jar chopped pimentos
1   4 ounce can mushroom pieces, chopped fine
1   can cream of mushroom soup
1   8 ounce carton sour cream
2   cups bread crumbs
3   tablespoons butter, melted
½   cup grated cheese

Combine first 4 ingredients in casserole. Stir in sour cream. Mix bread crumbs with butter in bowl. Sprinkle bread crumbs and cheese over broccoli. Bake at 350 degrees for 30 minutes. Makes 8 servings.

Nutritional Analysis Per Serving:

Calories:.........211.25		Vitamin C: ....56.75 mg	
Protein: ....7 g		Thiamine:.......... .11 mg	
Carbohydrates: .....13.75 g		Riboflavin: .... .26 mg	
Fat: ....15.25 g		Niacin: ....1.28 mg	
Phosphate: ....140.88 mg		Calcium: ....155 mg	
Potassium:........307.88 mg		Iron: ....1.25 mg	
Zinc: ....93 mg		Cholesterol:........32.75 mg	
Vitamin A: ....2865.88 iu		Sodium: ....510.75 mg	

Italian Broccoli Casserole

2   eggs, beaten
1   can cheddar cheese soup
½   teaspoon oregano
3   tablespoons parmesan cheese
2   cans tomato soup
2   10 ounce packages frozen chopped broccoli,
        cooked, drained

Combine all ingredients in bowl, mixing well. Pour into baking dish and top with cheese. Bake at 350 degrees for 30 minutes. Makes 6 servings.

Nutritional Analysis Per Serving:

Calories:	236.83	Vitamin C:	54.17 mg
Protein:	12.83 g	Thiamine:	.12 mg
Carbohydrates:	20.17 g	Riboflavin:	.35 mg
Fat:	12.67 g	Niacin:	1.47 mg
Phosphate:	384.67 mg	Calcium:	306.33 mg
Potassium:	467.83 mg	Iron:	1.6 mg
Zinc:	1.62 mg	Cholesterol:	104.67 mg
Vitamin A:	3230.83 iu	Sodium:	1394.33 mg

Broccoli Brown

1   10 ounce package frozen chopped broccoli, thawed and drained
4   eggs, beaten
2   cups milk
2   cups brown rice, cooked
1½   cups cheddar cheese, grated
4   green chilies, drained and finely chopped
½   teaspoon salt

Combine all ingredients, mixing well. Place in 2 quart baking dish. Bake at 350 degrees for 40 minutes. Let stand 10 minutes before serving. Makes 4 servings.

Nutritional Analysis Per Serving:

Calories:........... 437.5		Vitamin C:............ 47 mg	
Protein:............... 24 g		Thiamine:........... .23 mg	
Carbohydrates:..... 32.25 g		Riboflavin:........... .6 mg	
Fat:............... 23.75 g		Niacin:............. 1.85 mg	
Phosphate:....... 509.75 mg		Calcium:............ 521 mg	
Potassium:........ 575.25 mg		Iron:............... 2.3 mg	
Zinc:............... 3.13 mg		Cholesterol:......... 308 mg	
Vitamin A:.......... 2456 iu		Sodium:.......... 689.25 mg	

Broccoli Special

2   10 ounce packages frozen chopped broccoli
½   pound Velveeta cheese, cubed
½   stick butter

Cook broccoli for 5 minutes in boiling salted water. Drain, reserving ½ cup liquid. Place broccoli in baking dish. Pour reserved liquid over broccoli. Add cheese and ½ stick butter to broccoli. Bake at 350 degrees for 25 minutes. Makes 6 servings.

Nutritional Analysis Per Serving:

Calories: 260	Vitamin C: . . . . 39.5 mg
Protein: . . . . 8.33 g	Thiamine: . . . . .07 mg
Carbohydrates: . . . . 6.5 g	Riboflavin: . . . . .25 mg
Fat: . . . . 23.33 g	Niacin: . . . . .38 mg
Phosphate: . . . . 308.33 mg	Calcium: . . . . 251.67 mg
Potassium: . . . . 242.17 mg	Iron: . . . . .63 mg
Zinc: . . . . 1.18 mg	Cholesterol: . . . . 61.33 mg
Vitamin A: . . . . 2668.66 iu	Sodium: . . . . 666.83 mg

Broccoli-Rice Casserole

16   ounce package frozen chopped broccoli
¼   cup onion, finely chopped
¼   cup celery, finely chopped
4   tablespoons butter
1   can cream of chicken soup
1   can cream of mushroom soup
1   cup cheddar cheese, grated
1½   cups cooked rice

Cook broccoli according to package directions until tender. Saute onion and celery in butter. Combine soups and cheddar cheese; add onion and celery. Mix with broccoli. Season to taste. Add rice; pour into greased casserole. Bake at 350 degrees for 30 minutes. Makes 6 servings.

Nutritional Analysis Per Serving:

Calories: 301
Protein: . . . . 10.5 g
Carbohydrates: . . . . . 22.67 g
Fat: . . . . 19.33 g
Phosphate: . . . . 202.33 mg
Potassium: . . . . 271 mg
Zinc: . . . . 1.63 mg
Vitamin A: . . . . 2266.17 iu

Vitamin C: . . . . 36.33 mg
Thiamine: . . . . 12 mg
Riboflavin: . . . . 23 mg
Niacin: . . . . 1.32 mg
Calcium: . . . . 252.33 mg
Iron: . . . . 1.35 mg
Cholesterol: . . . . 45.67 mg
Sodium: . . . . 945.83 mg

Brussel Sprout Souffle

2	tablespoons butter
2	tablespoons grated parmesan cheese
10	ounce brussels sprouts, trimmed
1	medium sized potato, peeled and cubed
½	cup heavy cream
3	egg yolks
½	teaspoon salt
¼	teaspoon pepper
1/8	teaspoon ground nutmeg
	dash hot pepper sauce

Coat inside of 1 quart souffle dish with the butter. Sprinkle 1 teaspoon of the parmesan over bottom and sides of dish. To make collar for souffle, tear off a length of aluminum foil long enough to encircle dish. Fold in half lengthwise. Fasten collar to dish with string or tape so collar is 2 inches higher than rim.

Preheat oven to 400 degrees. Cook brussel sprouts and potato in boiling salted water to cover until tender, about 15 minutes. Drain.

Place half the brussel sprouts and half the potatoes in blender or food processor. Add ¼ cup of the cream. Whirl until smooth. Transfer to large bowl. Repeat with remaining brussel sprouts, potatoes and cream. Transfer to bowl and stir in remaining parmesan.

Beat egg yolks into brussel sprouts mixture one at a time, beating well after each addition. Stir in salt, pepper, nutmeg and hot pepper sauce.

Beat egg whites in medium-sized bowl until soft peaks form. Fold into brussel sprouts mixture until no streaks of white remain. Pour into prepared souffle dish. Place in hot oven and immediately lower temperature to 375 degrees and bake 35 minutes until puffed and golden. Makes 4 servings.

Nutritional Analysis Per Serving (continued on page 126)

125

Nutritional Analysis Per Serving:

Calories:. 258.5	Vitamin C:. . . . . .45 mg
Protein: . . . . .8.75 g	Thiamine:. . . . . .01 mg
Carbohydrates: . . . . . .9.25 g	Riboflavin: . . . . .23 mg
Fat:. . . . . .21.25 g	Niacin: . . . . .75 mg
Phosphate: . . . . . .144.75 mg	Calcium:. . . . . .89.75 mg
Potassium:. . . . . . . .315.75 mg	Iron: . . . . .1.23 mg
Zinc: . . . . .8 mg	Cholesterol:. . . . . . . .238.5 mg
Vitamin A: . . . . .1155.5 iu	Sodium: . . . . .463.5 mg

Carrot-Rice Casserole

3	cups carrots, shredded extra fine
⅔	cups rice
¼	teaspoon salt
2	cups cheddar cheese, shredded
1	can cream of celery soup
1	teaspoon onion, minced

Simmer carrots with rice and salt in 1½ cups water in saucepan for 25 minutes. Stir in 1½ cups cheese, soup, onion and ½ cup water. Spoon into 1½ quart casserole. Bake at 350 degrees for 1 hour. Top with remaining ½ cup cheese and bake for 2 minutes or until cheese melts. Makes 6 servings.

Nutritional Analysis Per Serving:

Calories:. 286.17	Vitamin C: . . . . .4.5 mg
Protein: . . . . .12.17 g	Thiamine:. . . . . .15 mg
Carbohydrates: . . . . .26.16 g	Riboflavin: . . . . .2 mg
Fat:. . . . . .14.83 g	Niacin: . . . . .1.13 mg
Phosphate: . . . . . . .250.67 mg	Calcium:. . . . . .3.22 mg
Potassium:. . . . . . . .268.17 mg	Iron: . . . . .1.52 mg
Zinc: . . . . .1.72 mg	Cholesterol:. . . . . . . .4.25 mg
Vitamin A: . . . . . . .8353.83 iu	Sodium: . . . . .754.5 mg

Carrot Puree

10	carrots, about 1½ pounds, cut into pieces
¼	cup butter, cut in pieces
1	teaspoon salt
¼	teaspoon black pepper
2	tablespoons heavy cream

Cook carrots in boiling salted water until tender; drain. Process carrots in food processor or blender. Add butter, salt and pepper. Process until smooth. Add cream and process until combined. To make an absolutely smooth puree, process an additional 30 seconds, then press through a fine sieve. Makes 4 servings.

Nutritional Analysis Per Serving:

Calories:	242.5	Vitamin C:	18.5 mg
Protein:	6.75 g	Thiamine:	.35 mg
Carbohydrates:	16.75 g	Riboflavin:	.015 mg
Fat:	17.25 g	Niacin:	2.18 mg
Phosphate:	123.5 mg	Calcium:	44.25 mg
Potassium:	246.75 mg	Iron:	2.48 mg
Zinc:	.95 mg	Cholesterol:	.51 mg
Vitamin A:	342.35 iu	Sodium:	268 mg

Carrot Pie

1   cup carrots, grated
3   eggs, separated
1   cup bread crumbs
½   cup milk
¼   cup onion, finely chopped
1   teaspoon salt
¼   teaspoon pepper

Beat egg yolks in a mixing bowl and add carrots, bread crumbs, milk, onion, salt and pepper. Beat egg whites until stiff peaks form. Fold egg whites into carrot mixture. Bake in 1½ quart casserole at 350 degrees for 30 minutes. Serves 6.

Nutritional Analysis Per Serving:

Calories:............103.5		Vitamin C: ....2.33 mg
Protein: ....7.5 g		Thiamine:...........0.05 mg
Carbohydrates: ......4.33 g		Riboflavin: ....0.15 mg
Fat:................6.17 g		Niacin: ....1.02 mg
Phosphate: ....101 mg		Calcium:............50.5 mg
Potassium:........168.33 mg		Iron: ....1.2 mg
Zinc: ....1.12 mg		Cholesterol:.......137.67 mg
Vitamin A: ....2792.5 iu		Sodium: ....66.33 mg

Cauliflower Puree

1   medium head cauliflower
2   teaspoons lemon juice
6   tablespoons butter, cut in pieces
1   teaspoon salt
1/8   teaspoon black pepper

Drain cauliflower in colander after cooking it in salted water until tender. Cool to room temperature, then cut in pieces. Process in food processor or blender with lemon juice. Add butter, salt and pepper. Process until smooth. Makes 4 servings.

Nutritional Analysis Per Serving (continued on page 129)

128

Nutritional Analysis Per Serving:

Calories:............164.5	Vitamin C:.............35 mg
Protein: ....1.75 g	Thiamine:.............05 mg
Carbohydrates: ....16 g	Riboflavin: ....05 mg
Fat:...............17.25 g	Niacin: ....38 mg
Phosphate: ....32 mg	Calcium: ....22 mg
Potassium: ....136 mg	Iron· ....48 mg
Zinc:.................3 mg	Cholesterol:........45.75 mg
Vitamin A: ....544.75 iu	Sodium:.............908 mg

Creamed Cauliflower

1	medium cauliflower, broken into florets
2	tablespoons butter
2	tablespoons flour
½	pint milk
	salt and pepper
	grated nutmeg

Cook cauliflower in lightly salted water until tender. Drain well. Melt the butter in pan and stir in flour. Cook for 1 minute, stirring, gradually add milk. Bring to a boil, stirring constantly, then season to taste with salt, pepper and nutmeg. Cook for 2 minutes. Blend cauliflower in blender until smooth, add white sauce. Sprinkle with nutmeg if desired. Makes 2 servings.

Nutritional Analysis Per Serving:

Calories:...........231.5	Vitamin C:.............70 mg
Protein: ....8 g	Thiamine:..............2 mg
Carbohydrates:........17 g	Riboflavin: ....35 mg
Fat:................15.5 g	Niacin: ....1.3 mg
Phosphate: ....176.5 mg	Calcium: ....176.5 mg
Potassium:........454.4 mg	Iron: ....1.25 mg
Zinc: ....1.1 mg	Cholesterol:........47.5 mg
Vitamin A:..........657 iu	Sodium:.............187 mg

Creamed Corn Casserole

3   16 ounce cans creamed corn
1   cup whipping cream
1   teaspoon salt
½   tablespoon butter
2   teaspoons flour
    parmesan cheese

Cook corn with whipping cream in saucepan until heated. Stir in salt. Melt butter and add flour, mixing well. Stir into corn and cook until slightly thick. Place corn mixture in casserole and top with parmesan cheese. Bake at 350 degrees for 25 minutes. Makes 10 servings.

Nutritional Analysis Per Serving:

Calories: 140	Vitamin C: . . . . 4.1 mg
Protein: . . . . 2.2 g	Thiamine: . . . . .03 mg
Carbohydrates: . . . . . . 16.5 g	Riboflavin: . . . . .07 mg
Fat: . . . . 8.4 g	Niacin: . . . . .8 mg
Phosphate: . . . . 58.6 mg	Calcium: . . . . 20.6 mg
Potassium: . . . . 98.4 mg	Iron: . . . . .48 mg
Zinc: . . . . .39 mg	Cholesterol: . . . . 28.1 mg
Vitamin A: . . . . 545.3 iu	Sodium: . . . . 427.7 mg

Corn Pudding

1   16 ounce can cream-style corn
½   teaspoon salt
3   eggs, slightly beaten
¼   teaspoon pepper
¼   teaspoon dry mustard
1   cup fine cracker crumbs
1   cup milk
1   teaspoon onion, minced
½   cup green pepper, finely chopped
2   ounce jar pimento, finely chopped
¼   cup butter

Mix all ingredients except butter in bowl, mixing well. Pour into greased casserole and dot with butter. Bake at 350 degrees for 1 hour. Makes 4 servings.

Nutritional Analysis Per Serving:

Calories: 360		Vitamin C: . . . . 43.25 mg	
Protein: . . . . 10.75 g		Thiamine: . . . . .2 mg	
Carbohydrates: . . . . . . 36.5 g		Riboflavin: . . . . .35 mg	
Fat: . . . . 20.5 g		Niacin: . . . . 1.93 mg	
Phosphate: . . . . 187.75 mg		Calcium: . . . . 121.25 mg	
Potassium: . . . . 322 mg		Iron: . . . . 2.58 mg	
Zinc: . . . . 1.18 mg		Cholesterol: . . . . 224 mg	
Vitamin A: . . . . 1092.5 iu		Sodium: . . . . 916 mg	

Green Beans Goldenrod

1   tablespoon butter, melted
1   tablespoon flour
¼   teaspoon salt
      dash of pepper
½   cup milk
2   hard-boiled eggs, separated, finely chopped
½   cup mayonnaise
1   can green beans, chopped
      paprika

Blend first 4 ingredients in saucepan and stir in milk. Cook until thick, stirring constantly; remove from heat. Add chopped egg white and mayonnaise. Cook green beans in saucepan until tender; drain. Place green beans in serving dish and top with sauce. Sprinkle with sieved egg yolks and paprika. Makes 4 servings.

Nutritional Analysis Per Serving:

Calories:	302.5	Vitamin C:	3 mg
Protein:	5.25 g	Thiamine:	.05 mg
Carbohydrates:	7.5 g	Riboflavin:	.15 mg
Fat:	28.75 g	Niacin:	.35 mg
Phosphate:	95.25 mg	Calcium:	86.5 mg
Potassium:	151.25 mg	Iron:	1.7 mg
Zinc:	.68 mg	Cholesterol:	148.25 mg
Vitamin A:	655 iu	Sodium:	572 mg

Green Bean Puff-Stuff

16   ounces green beans, chopped fine
1   teaspoon onion minced
2   tablespoons butter, melted
2   tablespoons flour
½   teaspoon salt
1/8   teaspoon marjoram
    dash of pepper
¾   cup milk
2   eggs, separated
½   cup sharp cheddar cheese, shredded

Drain beans, reserving ¼ cup liquid. Place beans in baking dish. In a sauce pan, saute onion in butter until tender. Stir in flour, ¼ teaspoon salt, marjoram and pepper. Add milk and reserved bean liquid, mixing well. Cook over medium heat until thick, stirring constantly. Pour over beans. Beat egg whites and ¼ teaspoon salt in bowl until stiff peaks form. Stir cheese into well-beaten egg yolks. Fold into egg whites. Spread egg mixture over bean mixture. Bake at 375 degrees for 20 minutes. Makes 4 servings.

Nutritional Analysis Per Serving:

Calories:	201.5	Vitamin C:	3.25 mg
Protein:	9.25 g	Thiamine:	1 mg
Carbohydrates:	9.25 g	Riboflavin:	25 mg
Fat:	14.5 g	Niacin:	5 mg
Phosphate:	178 mg	Calcium:	203.75 mg
Potassium:	183.75 mg	Iron:	1.78 mg
Zinc:	1.18 mg	Cholesterol:	159.75 mg
Vitamin A:	855.75 iu	Sodium:	649.25 mg

Scalloped Mushrooms

1   pound mushrooms, finely diced
¼   cup crackers, crushed
4   tablespoons butter, melted
1   cup whipping cream
         salt and paprika to taste
1   tablespoon margarine

Mix mushrooms, crackers, butter and whipping cream, mixing well. Place in casserole, sprinkle with salt and paprika. Dot with margarine. Bake at 350 degrees for 45 minutes. Makes 4 servings.

Nutritional Analysis Per Serving:

Calories:...........316.5		Vitamin C: ....1.75 mg	
Protein: ....2.75 g		Thiamine:........... .08 mg	
Carbohydrates:.........7 g		Riboflavin: .... .25 mg	
Fat: ....31.75 g		Niacin: ....1.7 mg	
Phosphate: ....84.75 mg		Calcium: ....45 mg	
Potassium:.........199.5 mg		Iron: .... .55 mg	
Zinc: .... .63 mg		Cholesterol:.........97.5 mg	
Vitamin A:..........1220 iu		Sodium:............179 mg	

Puree of Peas

3	10 ounce packages frozen peas
1	small carrot, cut in pieces
2	scallions, cut in halves
½	cup water
¼	teaspoon dried thyme leaves
4	tablespoons butter
¼	cup heavy cream
	salt and pepper to taste

Place peas, carrot, scallions, water and seasonings in a saucepan. Bring to a boil, then reduce heat and simmer, covered, until peas are tender. Drain and discard carrot and scallions. Add peas to food processor or blender and process until smooth. Add butter and heavy cream. Process again until combined. Add salt and pepper to taste. Transfer to baking dish and set in pan of hot water. Bake in pre-heated oven at 300 degrees until heated through, about 20 minutes. Dot with additional butter before serving. Makes 8 servings.

Nutritional Analysis Per Serving:

Calories:	121.25	Vitamin C:	9.25 mg
Protein:	3.38 g	Thiamine:	.18 mg
Carbohydrates:	.75 g	Riboflavin:	.08 mg
Fat:	8.63 g	Niacin:	1.09 mg
Phosphate:	61.75 mg	Calcium:	22.13 mg
Potassium:	123.38 mg	Iron:	1.24 mg
Zinc:	4.75 mg	Cholesterol:	25.5 mg
Vitamin A:	1711.75 iu	Sodium:	134 mg

Cheese and Spinach Casserole

1   pound carton cottage cheese
3   eggs
½   pound American cheese, grated
1   tablespoon butter, melted
2   10 ounce packages frozen chopped spinach,
           thawed and drained
3   tablespoons flour
         pinch of salt

*Combine cottage cheese, eggs, American cheese and
butter, mixing well. Add spinach, flour and salt, mixing
well. Pour into buttered casserole. Bake at 350 for 1
hour. Makes 8 servings.*

Nutritional Analysis Per Serving:

Calories:...........190.88		Vitamin C: ....15.75 mg
Protein: ....15.88 g		Thiamine:............09 mg
Carbohydrates: ......5.63 g		Riboflavin: ....28 mg
Fat:...............11.88 g		Niacin: ....55 mg
Phosphate: ....292.75 mg		Calcium:..........245.13 mg
Potassium:.........257.5 mg		Iron: ....1.75 mg
Zinc: ....1.59 mg		Cholesterol:.........94.5 mg
Vitamin A: ....5020.88 iu		Sodium: ....466.75 mg

Spinach and Rice Casserole

1   10 ounce package frozen chopped spinach,
      cooked and drained
1   cup rice, cooked
1   teaspoon finely grated onion
¼   pound sharp cheddar cheese, grated
4   tablespoons butter

Combine all ingredients in bowl, mixing well. Spoon into buttered 3 quart casserole. Bake at 275 degrees for 20 minutes. Makes 4 servings.

Nutritional Analysis Per Serving:

Calories: 277	Vitamin C: . . . . .12.25 mg
Protein: . . . . .10 g	Thiamine: . . . . .01 mg
Carbohydrates: . . . . .13.75 g	Riboflavin: . . . . .2 mg
Fat: . . . . .20.75 g	Niacin: . . . . .73 mg
Phosphate: . . . . .187.5 mg	Calcium: . . . . .282.25 mg
Potassium: . . . . .258 mg	Iron: . . . . .1.98 mg
Zinc: . . . . .1.45 mg	Cholesterol: . . . . .60 mg
Vitamin A: . . . . .5785.5 iu	Sodium: . . . . .322.75 mg

Spinach Casserole

3   10 ounce packages chopped spinach, thawed, well drained

1   pint sour cream

1   package dry onion soup mix

Combine all ingredients in bowl, mixing well. Spoon into casserole. Bake at 350 degrees for 30 minutes. Makes 6 servings.

Nutritional Analysis Per Serving:

Calories:	172.33	Vitamin C:	25.33 mg
Protein:	6.17 g	Thiamine:	.11 mg
Carbohydrates:	8.33 g	Riboflavin:	.28 mg
Fat:	14 g	Niacin:	.58 mg
Phosphate:	84.5 mg	Calcium:	220.5 mg
Potassium:	528.33 mg	Iron:	2.8 mg
Zinc:	.95 mg	Cholesterol:	30.83 mg
Vitamin A:	10627.33 iu	Sodium:	215.33 mg

Baked Spinach

2   eggs, slightly beaten
2   cups milk
1   teaspoon salt
2   10 ounce packages frozen chopped spinach,
       cooked and drained
2/3 cup bread crumbs
1½ cups cheddar cheese, grated

Combine eggs, milk and salt, mixing well. Stir in spinach, bread crumbs and ½ the cheese. Pour in casserole. Sprinkle remaining cheese around edge of casserole. Garnish with paprika. Bake at 375 for 40 minutes. Makes 8 servings.

Nutritional Analysis Per Serving:

Calories:	163.63	Vitamin C:	12.75 mg
Protein:	10.88 g	Thiamine:	.1 mg
Carbohydrates:	7.25 g	Riboflavin:	.31 mg
Fat:	10.63 g	Niacin:	.45 mg
Phosphate:	217.25 mg	Calcium:	308.75 mg
Potassium:	345.13 mg	Iron:	1.88 mg
Zinc:	1.46 mg	Cholesterol:	92.5 mg
Vitamin A:	5420.88 iu	Sodium:	516.88 mg

Spinach and Yogurt

1   pound frozen chopped spinach
5   ounces natural low-fat yogurt
1   clove garlic, crushed
    salt and pepper

Cook frozen spinach according to package instructions. Drain and cool. Mix yogurt and garlic and stir into spinach. Add salt and pepper to taste. Re-heat and serve. Makes 4 servings.

Nutritional Analysis Per Serving:

Calories:	42.25	Vitamin C:	25.5 mg
Protein:	5 g	Thiamine:	.08 mg
Carbohydrates:	6.25 g	Riboflavin:	.23 mg
Fat:	.25 g	Niacin:	.5 mg
Phosphate:	94.75 mg	Calcium:	160.25 mg
Potassium:	389.75 mg	Iron:	2.03 mg
Zinc:	1 mg	Cholesterol:	.75 mg
Vitamin A:	7292.5 iu	Sodium:	74.5 mg

Squash Casserole

5   yellow squash, finely chopped
1   onion, finely chopped
1   teaspoon salt
½   teaspoon pepper
½   stick margarine
1   cup grated cheese
1   slice bread, torn in small pieces

Cook squash and onion in a small amount of water until tender. Drain and mash. Add salt, pepper, margarine, cheese and bread; mix well. Pour into greased 1 quart baking dish. Bake at 350 degrees for 30 minutes. Makes 6 servings.

Nutritional Analysis Per Serving:

Calories:	181.17	Vitamin C:	16.17 mg
Protein:	6.67 g	Thiamine:	.1 mg
Carbohydrates:	8.17 g	Riboflavin:	.22 mg
Fat:	14.17 g	Niacin:	1.38 mg
Phosphate:	145.5 mg	Calcium:	186.17mg
Potassium:	256.67 mg	Iron:	.9 mg
Zinc:	1.03 mg	Cholesterol:	19.83 mg
Vitamin A:	1105.17 iu	Sodium:	617.83 mg

Squash Delight

1   large squash
1   green pepper, chopped
1   onion, chopped
¾   cup tomatoes, peeled and chopped
      parmesan cheese
      butter

Cook all ingredients in saucepan until soft. Place in blender until smooth. Re-heat and sprinkle with parmesan cheese and dot with butter. Makes 4 servings.

Nutritional Analysis Per Serving:

Calories:	208.25	Vitamin C:	10.13 mg
Protein:	5 g	Thiamine:	.08 mg
Carbohydrates:	17.5 g	Riboflavin:	.18 mg
Fat:	13.88 g	Niacin:	1.34 mg
Phosphate:	91.62 mg	Calcium:	81.88 mg
Potassium:	230.5 mg	Iron:	1.11 mg
Zinc:	.84 mg	Cholesterol:	48.13 mg
Vitamin A:	903.88 iu	Sodium:	585 mg

Squash Surprise

2½   pounds yellow squash, chopped
1   medium onion, chopped
½   stick margarine
1   can cream of chicken soup
1   cup sour cream
½   8 ounce package corn bread stuffing mix

Combine squash and onion with a small amount of water in saucepan. Cook until tender; drain and mash. Add remaining ingredients, mixing well. Spoon into casserole. Bake at 350 degrees for 30 minutes. Makes 8 servings.

Nutritional Analysis Per Serving:

Calories: 178	Vitamin C: . . . . 70.75 mg
Protein: . . . . 7.75 g	Thiamine: . . . . .1 mg
Carbohydrates: . . . . . 17.25 g	Riboflavin: . . . . .2 mg
Fat: . . . . 10 g	Niacin: . . . . 1.03 mg
Phosphate: . . . . 163 mg	Calcium: . . . . 208.5 mg
Potassium: . . . . 552.5 mg	Iron. . . . . 1.28 mg
Zinc: . . . . .8 mg	Cholesterol: . . . . .25 mg
Vitamin A: . . . . 3964.5 iu	Sodium: . . . . 299.25 mg

Wild Rice and Tomatoes

1	16 ounce package wild rice
½	pound mushrooms, finely chopped
½	cup onion, minced
¼	cup green pepper, finely chopped
¼	cup red pepper, finely chopped
19	ounce can tomatoes, finely chopped
½	pound mozzarella cheese, grated
1	teaspoon salt

Soak wild rice overnight; drain. Prepare rice according to package directions. Saute mushrooms, onion and peppers in a small amount of oil in skillet. Add tomatoes, cheese, salt and rice, mixing well. Place mixture in buttered 3 quart casserole. Bake at 350 degrees for 1 hour. Makes 8 servings.

Nutritional Analysis Per Serving:

Calories:	329.88	Vitamin C:	30.13 mg
Protein:	12 g	Thiamine:	.22 mg
Carbohydrates:	49 g	Riboflavin:	.2 mg
Fat:	9.5 g	Niacin:	3.35 mg
Phosphate:	280.75 mg	Calcium:	238.5 mg
Potassium:	383.5 mg	Iron:	1.5 mg
Zinc:	2.05 mg	Cholesterol:	26.25 mg
Vitamin A:	1199.88 iu	Sodium:	1023.13 mg

Tomato Aspic

1   3 ounce package lemon gelatin
1   can tomato soup
     juice of ½ lemon
     salt and pepper
     dash of worcestershire sauce

Dissolve gelatin in 1 cup boiling water in bowl. Stir in remaining ingredients. Chill until firm. Makes 4 servings.

Nutritional Analysis Per Serving:

Calories:	121.25	Vitamin C:	10 mg
Protein:	3 g	Thiamine:	.03 mg
Carbohydrates:	25.75 g	Riboflavin:	.03 mg
Fat:	1.5 g	Niacin:	.78 mg
Phosphate:	22 mg	Calcium:	9.5 mg
Potassium:	151.75 mg	Iron:	.48 mg
Zinc:	.13 mg	Cholesterol:	0 mg
Vitamin A:	628.75 iu	Sodium:	662.5 mg

Zucchini Au Gratin

4   medium zucchini
1   clove garlic, minced
1   small onion, minced
4   tablespoons oil
½   teaspoon salt
¼   teaspoon pepper
2   tablespoons parmesan cheese
¼   cup tomato sauce
3   slices swiss cheese

Saute zucchini, garlic and onion in oil in skillet for 5 minutes. Sprinkle with salt, pepper and parmesan cheese. Place in 1 quart casserole. Brush with tomato sauce and top with swiss cheese. Bake at 350 degrees for 15 minutes or until cheese melts. Makes 4 servings.

Nutritional Analysis Per Serving:

Calories: 252	Vitamin C: . . . . 24.5 mg
Protein: . . . . 9.25 g	Thiamine: . . . . .1 mg
Carbohydrates: . . . . . . 9.25 g	Riboflavin: . . . . .25 mg
Fat: . . . . 20.75 g	Niacin: . . . . 1.68 mg
Phosphate: . . . . 210.5 mg	Calcium: . . . . 291 mg
Potassium: . . . . 318 mg	Iron: . . . . .975 mg
Zinc: . . . . 1.43 mg	Cholesterol: . . . . 21.25 mg
Vitamin A: . . . . 1082.75 iu	Sodium: . . . . 486.5 mg

Zucchini Mexicali

2   pounds zucchini, cubed
½   cup milk
1   pound monterey jack cheese, grated
¼   cup parsley, finely chopped
1   4 ounce can finely chopped green chilies
3   tablespoons flour
4   eggs, beaten
1   teaspoon baking powder
1   cup bread crumbs
1   tablespoon butter

Boil the zucchini until tender. Layer in casserole with mixture consisting of milk, cheese, parsley, chilies, flour, egg and baking powder. Top with bread crumbs and butter. Bake 40 minutes at 325 degrees. Makes 8 servings.

Nutritional Analysis Per Serving:

Calories:	322.88	Vitamin C:	19 mg
Protein:	18.88 g	Thiamine:	.13 mg
Carbohydrates:	10 g	Riboflavin:	.41 mg
Fat:	23.25 g	Niacin:	1.23 mg
Phosphate:	380.63 mg	Calcium:	492.13 mg
Potassium:	311.13 mg	Iron:	1.63 mg
Zinc:	2.41 mg	Cholesterol:	188.13 mg
Vitamin A:	1361.75 iu	Sodium:	514.63 mg

Apple Cabbage

1	medium red cabbage, finely chopped
2	apples, grated
¼	cup onion, finely chopped
½	cup vinegar
½	cup water
½	cup honey
1	teaspoon salt
1	tablespoon butter
	dash of pepper

Mix all ingredients in a large pot. Bring to a boil and reduce heat. Simmer on low heat for 3 hours. Add water as needed. Serves 6.

Nutritional Analysis Per Serving:

Calories: 148	Vitamin C: . . . . 38.67 mg
Protein: . . . . 1.5 g	Thiamine: . . . . .07 mg
Carbohydrates: . . . . . 34.17 g	Riboflavin: . . . . .07 mg
Fat: . . . . 2.17 g	Niacin: . . . . .43 mg
Phosphate: . . . . 31.67 mg	Calcium: . . . . 59.17 mg
Potassium: . . . . 260.67 mg	Iron: . . . . .85 mg
Zinc: . . . . .57 mg	Cholesterol: . . . . .5 mg
Vitamin A: . . . . 237.67 iu	Sodium: . . . . 425.67 mg

Cucumber Filling

1   large cucumber, peeled, seeded, and cut
        into small pieces
6   parsley sprigs
1   small onion, halved
     salt and pepper to taste
     mayonnaise

Add cucumber, parsley, onion, salt and pepper to blender and process until very finely chopped. Stir in enough mayonnaise to bind. Spread on soft bread squares, which has had crust removed. Makes 4 servings.

Nutritional Analysis Per Serving:

Calories:	64	Vitamin C:	8 mg
Protein:	.75 g	Thiamine:	.03 mg
Carbohydrates:	3.25 g	Riboflavin:	.03 mg
Fat:	5.5 g	Niacin:	.13 mg
Phosphate:	1.7 mg	Calcium:	15.5 mg
Potassium:	104 mg	Iron:	.33 mg
Zinc:	.15 mg	Cholesterol:	4 mg
Vitamin A:	113 iu	Sodium:	44.5 mg

The Berries

1	cup strawberries
1	10 ounce package frozen raspberries, thawed
1½	cups cold milk
1	8 ounce container vanilla yogurt
2	eggs
¼	cup honey
½	teaspoon vanilla extract

Place strawberries, raspberries and ½ cup milk in a blender container. Blend on high speed for 1 minute or until smooth. Add remaining milk and other ingredients. Blend until frothy. Serve immediately in tall, chilled glass. Makes 3 servings.

Nutritional Analysis Per Serving:

Calories:	426	Vitamin C:	49.33 mg
Protein:	13.33 g	Thiamine:	17 mg
Carbohydrates:	83.67 g	Riboflavin:	.6 mg
Fat:	6.33 g	Niacin:	1.2 mg
Phosphate:	326.33 mg	Calcium:	352.67 mg
Potassium:	629.33mg	Iron:	2.1 mg
Zinc:	2.2 mg	Cholesterol:	175.67 mg
Vitamin A:	500.67 iu	Sodium:	169.67 mg

Fresh Applesauce

4   apples
¼   cup water
2   tablespoons lemon juice
6   packets of Equal®

Peel, core, and cube apples. Place all ingredients in blender and blend until smooth. Serve immediately. Makes 4 servings.

Nutritional Analysis Per Serving:

Calories:............87.5	Vitamin C: ....8.75 mg
Protein: .... .25 g	Thiamine:........... .05 mg
Carbohydrates:........22 g	Riboflavin: .... .02 mg
Fat:................ .75 g	Niacin: .... .01 mg
Phosphate: ....14.5 mg	Calcium: ....10 mg
Potassium:........162.25 mg	Iron: .... .42 mg
Zinc: .... .07 mg	Cholesterol: ....0 mg
Vitamin A: ....125.5 iu	Sodium: ....1.25 mg

Tapioca Pudding

3   tablespoons minute tapioca
4   tablespoons honey
2   cups milk
2   eggs, separated
1   tablespoon vanilla extract
1   packet of Equal"
     dash salt

Mix tapioca, salt, 3 tablespoons honey, milk and egg yolks in heavy saucepan. Let stand 5 minutes. Bring to full boil, stirring constantly, over medium heat, 8 to 10 minutes. Remove from heat.

Beat egg whites until foamy; gradually beat in 1 packet Equal® until whites stand in soft peaks. Fold egg whites into warm tapioca. Add vanilla. Stir and serve warm; or chill and serve cold. Makes 4 servings.

Nutritional Analysis Per Serving:

Calories: 202	Vitamin C: . . . . .1.5 mg
Protein: . . . . .6.75 g	Thiamine: . . . . .0.08 mg
Carbohydrates: . . . . .30.25 g	Riboflavin: . . . . .0.28 mg
Fat: . . . . .6.5 g	Niacin: . . . . .0.2 mg
Phosphate: . . . . .157 mg	Calcium: . . . . .160 mg
Potassium: . . . . .227.5 mg	Iron: . . . . .0.73 mg
Zinc: . . . . .0.8 mg	Cholesterol: . . . . . . .140.25 mg
Vitamin A: . . . . .271.25 iu	Sodium: . . . . .92.25 mg

Orange Pudding Cake

½   cup honey
2   tablespoons butter
1½   tablespoons orange rind, grated
4   eggs, separated
¼   cup flour
1   cup milk
½   cup orange juice
8   packets of Equal®

Mix ½ cup honey, butter and orange rind together. Add egg yolks one at a time, beating well after each addition. Add flour, milk and orange juice gradually. Beat egg whites in separate bowl, add 8 packets of Equal® and beat until stiff. Fold into orange mixture. Place mixture in buttered casserole and bake at 350 degrees for 1 hour. Makes 4 servings.

Nutritional Analysis Per Serving:

Calories:	341	Vitamin C:	19.75 mg
Protein:	9.25 g	Thiamine:	0.15 mg
Carbohydrates:	48.5 g	Riboflavin:	0.33 mg
Fat:	13.5 g	Niacin:	0.8 mg
Phosphate:	168.5 mg	Calcium:	127.75 mg
Potassium:	271.75 mg	Iron:	1.55 mg
Zinc:	1.03 mg	Cholesterol:	272.5 mg
Vitamin A:	608 iu	Sodium:	160 mg

Chocolate Velvet Pudding Pie

1   3½ ounce package chocolate instant pudding
       and pie filling
1   cup cold milk
2   squares semi-sweet chocolate, melted
1   8 ounce carton non-dairy whipped topping,
       thawed

Prepare pudding with 1 cup milk as directed on package, with electric mixer. Gradually blend in chocolate at low speed until smooth. Then fold in whipped topping. Spoon into dessert glasses and freeze until firm, about 4 hours. Makes 4 servings.

Nutritional Analysis Per Serving:

Calories:...........322.5		Vitamin C: ....1.25 mg
Protein: ....4.75 g		Thiamine:........... .05 mg
Carbohydrates: .....46.25 g		Riboflavin: .... .2 mg
Fat:...............15.25 g		Niacin: .... .2 mg
Phosphate: ....141.5 mg		Calcium: ....193 mg
Potassium:........218.25 mg		Iron: ....1.05 mg
Zinc: .... .5 mg		Cholesterol:........14.25 mg
Vitamin A: ....412.75 iu		Sodium: ....168.25 mg

Rice Pudding

1   tablespoon cornstarch
1½ tablespoons honey
1   egg, beaten
1   cup milk
½   cup rice, well cooked
½   teaspoon vanilla

Blend first three ingredients in saucepan until smooth. Add milk slowly, stirring to mix well. Add rice. Cook over medium heat, stirring constantly until mixture is thick and comes to a boil. Remove from heat, add vanilla and cool. Sprinkle with cinnamon and nutmeg, if desired. Serve warm. Makes 4 servings.

Nutritional Analysis Per Serving:

Calories:.........110.75	Vitamin C: .... .75 mg
Protein: ....3.75 g	Thiamine: .... .05 mg
Carbohydrates: .....16.75 g	Riboflavin:.......... .13 mg
Fat:................3.25 g	Niacin:............. .33 mg
Phosphate: ....83.75 mg	Calcium:...........81.75 mg
Potassium: ....118 mg	Iron: .... .55 mg
Zinc:.............. .50 mg	Cholesterol: ....70 mg
Vitamin A: ....135.5 iu	Sodium: ....45.75 mg

Vanilla Pudding

¼   cup honey
2   tablespoons cornstarch
2   cups milk
1   egg, beaten
1   teaspoon vanilla

Place honey and cornstarch in saucepan. Add milk. Add beaten egg. Cook over medium heat until thick and comes to a boil. Add vanilla and cool. Makes 4 servings.

Nutritional Analysis Per Serving:

Calories: 172	Vitamin C: . . . . 1.5 mg
Protein: . . . . 5.5 g	Thiamine: . . . . .05 mg
Carbohydrates: . . . . . 26.75 g	Riboflavin: . . . . .25 mg
Fat: . . . . 5.25 g	Niacin: . . . . .20 mg
Phosphate: . . . . 135.25 mg	Calcium: . . . . 153 mg
Potassium: . . . . 211.5 mg	Iron: . . . . .48 mg
Zinc: . . . . .65 mg	Cholesterol: . . . . 78.75 mg
Vitamin A: . . . . 212.75 iu	Sodium: . . . . 76.5 mg

Creamy Banana Pudding

3   cups milk
3   large egg yolks
⅓   cup honey
3   tablespoons cornstarch
1½   teaspoons vanilla extract
2   large ripe bananas
      few grains of salt

Put all ingredients except bananas in a 3 quart saucepan and whisk until thoroughly blended. Stir 6 to 7 minutes over moderate heat, until mixture thickens and comes to a boil. Reduce heat to low and cook 1 minute, stirring constantly. Remove from heat and stir in bananas. Serve warm or chilled. Makes 6 servings.

Nutritional Analysis Per Serving:

Calories: 216	Vitamin C: . . . . 6 mg
Protein: . . . . 6 g	Thiamine: . . . . 1 mg
Carbohydrates: . . . . . 34.67 g	Riboflavin: . . . . .27 mg
Fat: . . . . 7 g	Niacin: . . . . .5 mg
Phosphate: . . . . .170 mg	Calcium: . . . . 163.17 mg
Potassium: . . . . .371 mg	Iron: . . . . 1.02 mg
Zinc: . . . . .87 mg	Cholesterol: . . . . 153.17 mg
Vitamin A: . . . . .396.67 iu	Sodium: . . . . .65.5 mg

Cherry Angel Dessert

8   cups angel food cake, cut in small cubes
1   21 ounce can cherry pie filling
1   package instant vanilla pudding
1½   cups milk
1   cup dairy sour cream

Place half of the cake cubes in a 9x13x2 inch pan. Reserve ⅓ cup cherry pie filling for topping. Spoon remaining pie filling over cubes. Top with remaining cubes. Combine milk, ⅓ cup remaining cherry filling, sour cream and beat until smooth. Spoon over the top. Cover and refrigerate. Makes 8 servings.

Nutritional Analysis Per Serving:

Calories:	367	Vitamin C:	3.38 mg
Protein:	7.75 g	Thiamine:	.11 mg
Carbohydrates:	71.38 g	Riboflavin:	.28 mg
Fat:	7 g	Niacin:	.79 mg
Phosphate:	103.25 mg	Calcium:	139 mg
Potassium:	273.5 mg	Iron:	1.01 mg
Zinc:	.49 mg	Cholesterol:	17.63 mg
Vitamin A:	322.75 iu	Sodium:	263.88 mg

Chocolate Bread Pudding

4	eggs
2¾	cups milk, scalded
2	cups bread crumbs
1	square unsweetened chocolate, melted
⅔	cup honey
8	packets Equal®
1	teaspoon vanilla extract

Mix 2 eggs with milk, bread crumbs, chocolate and ⅔ cup honey. Pour into greased casserole and bake at 325 degrees for 45 minutes. Separate remaining 2 eggs. Add 8 packets Equal® to stiffly beaten egg whites. Add vanilla and egg yolks. Top warm pudding with egg mixture. Makes 6 servings.

Nutritional Analysis Per Serving:

Calories: 298	Vitamin C: . . . . 1.67 mg
Protein: . . . . 9.33 g	Thiamine: . . . . .13 mg
Carbohydrates: . . . . . 45.83 g	Riboflavin: . . . . .35 mg
Fat: . . . . 10.33 g	Niacin: . . . . .75 mg
Phosphate: . . . . 200.17 mg	Calcium: . . . . 178.5 mg
Potassium: . . . . 296 mg	Iron: . . . . 1.56 mg
Zinc: . . . . 1.05 mg	Cholesterol: . . . . 181.83 mg
Vitamin A: . . . . 313 iu	Sodium: . . . . 166.83 mg

Honey Baked Custard

3   eggs
¼   tablespoon salt
2   cups milk
4   tablespoons honey

Scald milk; then stir in the honey. Beat eggs and salt together. Stir in a small amount of hot milk mixture into egg mixture. Stir egg mixture into hot milk. Pour into 6 custard cups. Place in pan of hot water and bake for 30 minutes in 375 degree oven. Chill and serve cold. Serves 6.

Nutritional Analysis Per Serving:

Calories: 118	Vitamin C: . . . . .1 mg
Protein: . . . . .5.33 g	Thiamine: . . . . .05 mg
Carbohydrates: . . . . .15.67 g	Riboflavin: . . . . .20 mg
Fat: . . . . .4 g	Niacin: . . . . .15 mg
Phosphate: . . . . .118.5 mg	Calcium: . . . . .116.33 mg
Potassium: . . . . .161.33 mg	Iron: . . . . .62 mg
Zinc: . . . . .65 mg	Cholesterol: . . . . . . .126.33 mg
Vitamin A: . . . . .281.33 iu	Sodium: . . . . .648.5 mg

Bread and Butter Pudding

10	slices white bread, trimmed
8	tablespoons butter
4	eggs
2	egg yolks
2/3	cup honey
1/8	teaspoon salt
2	cups milk
1	cup cream
1	teaspoon vanilla extract
1/3	cup sifted confectioners' sugar

Heavily butter the inside of a 2 quart baking dish. Butter each slice of bread. Arrange bread in several layers, butter side up, across bottom of pan, cutting slices to fill in any large gaps.

Beat together eggs, yolks, honey, and salt. Scald milk and cream together, add to egg mixture, and add vanilla. Pour over bread in baking dish. Let sit for 20 minutes.

Preheat oven to 325 degrees. Set baking dish in a large pan in about 1 inch of hot water. Bake 1½ hours.

Put under hot broiler for a few minutes to glaze. Watch carefully to make sure it does not burn. Makes 8 servings.

Nutritional Analysis Per Serving:

Calories:. 436.5		Vitamin C:. . . . . .1 mg
Protein: . . . . .8.8 g		Thiamine: . . . . .2 mg
Carbohydrates: . . . . . .36.3 g		Riboflavin:. . . . . .3 mg
Fat:. . . . . .29.3 g		Niacin: . . . . .1.2 mg
Phosphate: . . . . .169.5 mg		Calcium:. . . . . .141.3 mg
Potassium:. . . . . .191.8 mg		Iron: . . . . .1.6 mg
Zinc:. . . . . .9 mg		Cholesterol:. . . . . . . .264.6 mg
Vitamin A: . . . . .1132.3 iu		Sodium: . . . . .397.6 mg

Nectarine Orange Ice

4   large fresh nectarines
4   medium oranges
12   packets of Equal®
      mint sprigs, optional

Puree, in food processor or blender, nectarines to measure 2½ cups. Cut oranges in half and squeeze juice to make 1 cup. Remove pulp from orange shells; slice a thin strip from bottom so each will stand evenly; wrap shells and freeze. In a large bowl, combine nectarine puree and orange juice with Equal® . Cover and freeze until solid. Remove nectarine-orange ice from freezer and let stand until you can break ice into pieces. With an electric mixer, whip ice until smooth and thick like cake batter. Cover and refreeze until solid. To serve, let stand at room temperature until it's soft enough to scoop, about 10 minutes. Mound scoops of softened ice into frozen orange shells; garnish with mint sprig, if desired. Makes 4 servings.

Nutritional Analysis Per Serving:

Calories:.........169.75	Vitamin C: ....89.5 mg
Protein: ....2.25 g	Thiamine: .... .17 mg
Carbohydrates:.......44 g	Riboflavin:.......... .12 mg
Fat:............... .25 g	Niacin: ....1.95 mg
Phosphate: ....61.5 mg	Calcium: ....64 mg
Potassium:........691.75 mg	Iron: ....1.27 mg
Zinc:............... .04 mg	Cholesterol: ....0 mg
Vitamin A:.........2563 iu	Sodium: ....9.5 mg

Lime Banana Ice

½   cup water
¼   cup fresh lime juice
1   tablespoon honey
¼   teaspoon grated fresh lime peel
2   very ripe bananas, peeled
    dash ground nutmeg

Combine water, lime juice, honey, lime peel and nutmeg in saucepan. Simmer 5 minutes; strain. Cool. Combine with bananas; puree in food processor or blender until smooth. Pour into 9 inch square metal pan. Cover and freeze until slushy. Place in chilled mixing bowl; beat until airy. Return to freezer until set but not hard. Before serving, scrape surface with spoon to resemble crushed ice. Serve immediately. Makes 1 serving.

Nutritional Analysis Per Serving:

Calories: 282	Vitamin C: . . . . 37 mg
Protein: . . . . 3 g	Thiamine: . . . . .1 mg
Carbohydrates: . . . . 76 g	Riboflavin: . . . . .2 mg
Fat: . . . . .1 g	Niacin: . . . . 1.8 mg
Phosphate: . . . . 69 mg	Calcium: . . . . 25 mg
Potassium: . . . . 955 mg	Iron: . . . . 1.9 mg
Zinc: . . . . .5 mg	Cholesterol: . . . . .0 mg
Vitamin A: . . . . 4.58 iu	Sodium: . . . . .4 mg

Fresh Plum and Strawberry Ice

1½   pounds fresh plums
1   pint strawberries, hulled
12   packets of Equal®
½   cup water
1   tablespoon lemon juice

Halve plums and remove pits. Combine plums, strawberries, and water in saucepan. Bring to a boil, cover and simmer 5 minutes or until plums are tender. Cool. Whirl with lemon juice in electric blender until smooth. Let cool, add 12 packets of Equal . Pour into a 6 cup freezer container and place in freezer until firm, stirring every 30 minutes. Makes 6 servings.

Nutritional Analysis Per Serving:

Calories: 57	Vitamin C: . . . . .37.8 mg
Protein: . . . . .6 g	Thiamine: . . . . .02 mg
Carbohydrates: . . . . . .14.2 g	Riboflavin: . . . . .06 mg
Fat: . . . . .4 g	Niacin: . . . . .52 mg
Phosphate: . . . . .18.8 mg	Calcium: . . . . .16.6 mg
Potassium: . . . . .159 mg	Iron: . . . . .78 mg
Zinc: . . . . .06 mg	Cholesterol: . . . . .0 mg
Vitamin A: . . . . .486.6 iu	Sodium: . . . . .80 mg

Strawberry Ice

4   cups fresh strawberries
½   cup unsweetened orange juice
3   tablespoons honey

Combine all ingredients in blender and blend until smooth. Pour mixture into 8 inch square pan and freeze until slushy. Spoon into blender and process until smooth. Freeze until firm. Makes 4 servings.

Nutritional Analysis Per Serving:

Calories: 117	Vitamin C: . . . . 103.75 mg
Protein: . . . . 1.25 g	Thiamine: . . . . .08 mg
Carbohydrates: . . . . 28.75 g	Riboflavin: . . . . .13 mg
Fat: . . . . .75 g	Niacin: . . . . 1.08 mg
Phosphate: . . . . 37.5 mg	Calcium: . . . . 35.5 mg
Potassium: . . . . 314.75 mg	Iron: . . . . 1.63 mg
Zinc: . . . . .15 mg	Cholesterol: . . . . .0 mg
Vitamin A: . . . . 151.75 iu	Sodium: . . . . 2.5 mg

166

Orange Ice

1   2 inch square orange peel
4½ cups freshly squeezed orange juice
18 packets of Equal®

Add orange peel, 1 cup orange juice and Equal® to food processor or blender. Process until combined. Add processed ingredients to remaining 3½ cups orange juice and mix well. Pour into 2 ice trays and freeze.

Just before serving add frozen cubes, one tray at a time to food processor or blender. Process until a fine ice is formed. Served immediately. Makes 4 servings.

Nutritional Analysis Per Serving:

Calories:	144	Vitamin C:	141.25 mg
Protein:	2 g	Thiamine:	.25 mg
Carbohydrates:	33.75 g	Riboflavin:	.07 mg
Fat:	.5 g	Niacin:	1.12 mg
Phosphate:	47.75 mg	Calcium:	31.5 mg
Potassium:	563.25 mg	Iron:	.57 mg
Zinc:	.05 mg	Cholesterol:	0 mg
Vitamin A:	562.75 iu	Sodium:	2.75 mg

Fruit Delight

2   15¼ ounce cans crushed pineapple, drained
1   16 ounce can pears, chopped fine
1   16 ounce can peaches, chopped fine
1   16 ounce can apricots, chopped fine
1   6 ounce jar maraschino cherries, drained and
        chopped fine
½   cup honey
½   teaspoon cloves
½   teaspoon allspice
¼   teaspoon cinnamon
½   stick butter, melted

Combine fruit in baking dish. Mix honey and spices with butter. Pour over fruit and bake at 350 degrees for 30 minutes. Makes 12 servings.

Nutritional Analysis Per Serving:

Calories:.........215.33	Vitamin C: ....8.33 mg
Protein: .... .67 g	Thiamine: .... .08 mg
Carbohydrates: .....47.75 g	Riboflavin:.......... .05 mg
Fat: ....4 g	Niacin:.............. .6 mg
Phosphate: ....18 mg	Calcium: ....17 mg
Potassium: ....227 mg	Iron:............... .61 mg
Zinc:.............. .21 mg	Cholesterol:........10.17 mg
Vitamin A:..........655 iu	Sodium: ....41.67 mg

Fruit Milk Sherbet

1½ cups of any fruit
2   tablespoons honey
1   teaspoon plain gelatin powder
1   teaspoon water
¾   cup milk
1   egg white

Puree fruit in blender. Soften the gelatin in water and blend into puree. Add honey and milk and blend thoroughly. Pour mixture into bowl, cover and freeze. When frozen, place mixture in blender until smooth. Fold in egg white. Return to bowl and re-freeze. Makes 2 servings.

Nutritional Analysis Per Serving:

Calories:. 173.5	Vitamin C: . . . . 67 mg
Protein: . . . . 7 g	Thiamine: . . . . .05 mg
Carbohydrates:. . . . . . . 31 g	Riboflavin: . . . . .3 mg
Fat: . . . . 3.5 g	Niacin: . . . . .85 mg
Phosphate: . . . . 111.5 mg	Calcium:. . . . . 135.5 mg
Potassium:. . . . . 353.5 mg	Iron: . . . . 1.3 mg
Zinc: . . . . .45 mg	Cholesterol: . . . . 12.5 mg
Vitamin A: . . . . 182.5 iu	Sodium: . . . . 70.5 mg

Pineapple-Mint Sherbet

1   10 ounce can crushed pineapple with juice
8   packets of Equal®
2   drops mint extract
2   egg whites

Drain pineapple in strainer set over large measuring cup; press well to remove juice. In medium-size saucepan heat ½ cup of juice; stir in drained pineapple and mint extract. Pour into 9x9x2 inch square baking pan. Freeze 45 minutes, stirring occasionally, just until slushy. In medium size bowl, with electric mixer at high speed, adding Equal® , beat egg whites until stiff peaks form when beaters are lifted. Stir semi-frozen pineapple into egg whites; beat mixture with electric mixer at high speed until frothy. Return to baking pan; freeze 1½ hours, stirring occasionally, until just firm enough to scoop. Makes 9 one-third cup servings.

Nutritional Analysis Per Serving:

Calories:...........32.77	Vitamin C: ....2.44 mg
Protein: .... .77 g	Thiamine: .... .03 mg
Carbohydrates: ......7.77 g	Riboflavin:.......... .02 mg
Fat: ....0 g	Niacin:............. .07 mg
Phosphate: ....2.44 mg	Calcium:...........4.55 mg
Potassium:.........42.77 mg	Iron: .... .11 mg
Zinc:............... .03 mg	Cholesterol: ....0 mg
Vitamin A: ....17.66 iu	Sodium: ....10.11 mg

Instant Mousse

1   3½ ounce package chocolate instant pudding
       and pie filling
1½   cups milk
1   cup thawed whipped topping

Prepare pudding mix, using 1½ cups milk. Fold in whipped topping and spoon into dessert dishes. Garnish with additional whipped topping. Makes 4 servings.

Nutritional Analysis Per Serving:

Calories:	251.5	Vitamin C:	1.25 mg
Protein:	4.25 g	Thiamine:	.05 mg
Carbohydrates:	38.25 g	Riboflavin:	.2 mg
Fat:	10.25 g	Niacin:	13 mg
Phosphate:	120.5 mg	Calcium:	188.75 mg
Potassium:	172.5 mg	Iron:	.68 mg
Zinc:	.45 mg	Cholesterol:	14.25 mg
Vitamin A:	410 iu	Sodium:	168 mg

Maple-Pumpkin Pie

½   of 11 ounce package pie crust mix
2   eggs
1   pound can pumpkin
½   cup honey
¼   cup maple syrup
1   teaspoon ground cinnamon
½   teaspoon salt
½   teaspoon ground ginger
¼   teaspoon ground cloves
1⅔   cups half and half
1   cup whipped cream

Prepare pie crust mix following lable directions for 9 inch pastry shell. Beat eggs slightly in large bowl. Beat in pumpkin, honey, maple syrup, cinnamon, salt, ginger and cloves, mixing well. Stir in half and half. Pour pumpkin mixture into pie shell. Bake at 425 degrees for 15 minutes. Cover with aluminum foil, reduce heat to 350 degrees and bake for another 55 minutes. Top with whipped cream. Makes 8 servings.

Nutritional Analysis Per Serving:

Calories: 324.12	Vitamin C: . . . . .3.75 mg
Protein: . . . . .5.12 g	Thiamine: . . . . .11 mg
Carbohydrates: . . . . .37.62 g	Riboflavin: . . . . .2 mg
Fat: . . . . .18.25 g	Niacin: . . . . .1.12 mg
Phosphate: . . . . .97.37 mg	Calcium: . . . . .79.87 mg
Potassium: . . . . .251.5 mg	Iron: . . . . .1.03 mg
Zinc: . . . .,67 mg	Cholesterol: . . . . .80 mg
Vitamin A: . . . . . . .4331.12 iu	Sodium: . . . . .468.37 mg

Vanilla Custard La Marmite

2¼   cups milk
1   four inch vanilla bean
5   large egg yolks
½   cup honey
3   tablespoons cornstarch

In a saucepan scald the milk with the vanilla bean and remove the bean. In a bowl beat the yolks until they are combined, beat in honey and cornstarch, and whisk in the milk in a stream. Transfer the mixture to a saucepan and cook it over moderate heat, stirring constantly, until it thickens. Simmer the mixture for 1 minute, strain it into a bowl, and cover it with a buttered round of wax paper. The custard keeps, covered and chilled, for 2 days. Makes 4 servings.

Nutritional Analysis Per Serving:

Calories: 313	Vitamin C: . . . . .1.75 mg
Protein: . . . . .8.25 g	Thiamine: . . . . .1 mg
Carbohydrates: . . . . .46.75 g	Riboflavin: . . . . .33 mg
Fat: . . . . .11.5 g	Niacin: . . . . .28 mg
Phosphate: . . . . .238.5 mg	Calcium: . . . . .198.25 mg
Potassium: . . . . .250 mg	Iron: . . . . .1.55 mg
Zinc: . . . . .1.28 mg	Cholesterol: . . . . .359.5 mg
Vitamin A: . . . . .564.25 iu	Sodium: . . . . .80 mg

Peanut Butter Custard

1⅓   cups milk
⅓   cup creamy peanut butter
2   eggs, beaten
3   tablespoons honey

Add milk to peanut butter, stirring until smooth. Blend in eggs and honey. Pour mixture into custard cups. Place cups in hot water to level of custard. Bake for 30 minutes at 325 degrees. Refrigerate and serve chilled. Makes 4 servings.

Nutritional Analysis Per Serving:

Calories: 240.75	Vitamin C: . . . . 1 mg
Protein: . . . . 11.25 g	Thiamine: . . . . .08 mg
Carbohydrates: . . . . . . 16.5 g	Riboflavin: . . . . .23 mg
Fat: . . . . 15.75 g	Niacin: . . . . .3.48 mg
Phosphate: . . . . 203.5 mg	Calcium: . . . . 123.25 mg
Potassium: . . . . .301 mg	Iron: . . . . 1.03 mg
Zinc: . . . . .1.25 mg	Cholesterol: . . . . .134.5 mg
Vitamin A: . . . . .219.5 iu	Sodium: . . . . .200.5 mg

Blender Bavarian Cream

2	envelopes unflavored gelatin
¾	cup hot water
1	package semi-sweet chocolate pieces
2	egg yolks
1	cup heavy cream
½	teaspoon vanilla
1	heaping cup crushed ice
	sweetened whipped cream and chocolate curls for garnish

Combine gelatin and hot water in electric blender. Cover; whirl at high speed, scraping down sides once, for 40 seconds. Add chocolate pieces. Cover; whirl 10 seconds. Add egg yolks, heavy cream, vanilla and crushed ice. Cover; blend at medium speed until ice dissolves and mixture begins to thicken.

Pour immediately into 6 dessert glasses. Chill until serving time, about 15 minutes. Garnish with sweetened whipped cream and chocolate curls. Makes 6 servings.

Nutritional Analysis Per Serving:

Calories:	395	Vitamin C:	.33 mg
Protein:	27.16 g	Thiamine:	.01 mg
Carbohydrates:	17.33 g	Riboflavin:	.08 mg
Fat:	26.66 g	Niacin:	.01 mg
Phosphate:	92.66 mg	Calcium:	45.16 mg
Potassium:	132.66 mg	Iron:	1.01 mg
Zinc:	.46 mg	Cholesterol:	134.83 mg
Vitamin A:	685.5 iu	Sodium:	43.66 mg

Banana — Egg Yoke Custard

1   banana
1   egg yolk
¼   cup milk

Blend together banana, egg yolk, and milk. Pour into custard cups and place in pan of water. Bake for 30 minutes in oven at 350 degrees. Refrigerate and serve chilled. Makes 1 servings.

Nutritional Analysis Per Serving:

Calories: 193		Vitamin C: . . . . 13 *mg*	
Protein: . . . . 6 *g*		Thiamine: . . . . .1 *mg*	
Carbohydrates: . . . . 29 *g*		Riboflavin: . . . . .2 *mg*	
Fat: . . . . 7 *g*		Niacin: . . . . .9 *mg*	
Phosphate: . . . . 164 *mg*		Calcium: . . . . 105 *mg*	
Potassium: . . . . 546 *mg*		Iron: . . . . 1.7 *mg*	
Zinc: . . . . 1.0 *mg*		Cholesterol: . . . . 248 *mg*	
Vitamin A. . . . . 579 *iu*		Sodium: . . . . 38 *mg*	

Coffee Pastry Cream

2	cups milk
1½	teaspoons instant coffee
10	packets of Equal®
4	egg yolks
½	cup flour
½	teaspoon cornstarch
½	teaspoon vanilla

Heat milk and instant coffee in saucepan, stirring to dissolve coffee. Put egg yolks in another saucepan. Add flour and cornstarch and mix thoroughly. Place over low heat and gradually add hot milk mixture, stirring continuously. Cool, stirring, until smooth and thick. Remove from heat, cool, add vanilla and Equal® . Makes 5 servings.

Nutritional Analysis Per Serving:

Calories:	174	Vitamin C:	1 mg
Protein:	6.6 g	Thiamine:	˙ .08 mg
Carbohydrates:	19 g	Riboflavin:	.22 mg
Fat:	7.6 g	Niacin:	.22 mg
Phosphate:	162.8 mg	Calcium:	136.8 mg
Potassium:	171.6 mg	Iron:	.88 mg
Zinc:	.86 mg	Cholesterol:	205.8 mg
Vitamin A:	344 iu	Sodium:	54 mg

Burnt Creme

1   pint whipping cream
4   egg yolks
½   cup honey
1   tablespoon vanilla extract

Preheat oven to 350 degrees. Heat cream over low heat until bubbles form around edge of pan. Beat egg yolks and honey together until thick, about 3 minutes. Gradually beat cream into egg yolks. Stir in vanilla and pour into 6 (6 ounce) custard cups. Place custard cups n baking pan that has about ½ inch water in the bottom. Bake until set, about 45 minutes. Remove custard cups from water and refrigerate until chilled. Place on top rack under broiler and cook until topping is medium brown. Chill before serving. Makes 6 servings.

Nutritional Analysis Per Serving:

Calories: 431		Vitamin C: . . . . .1 mg	
Protein: . . . . .3.33 g		Thiamine: . . . . .05 mg	
Carbohydrates: . . . . .33.83 g		Riboflavin: . . . . .15 mg	
Fat: . . . . .32.83 g		Niacin: . . . . .1 mg	
Phosphate: . . . . .102 mg		Calcium: . . . . .68.5 mg	
Potassium: . . . . .83.5 mg		Iron: . . . . .72 mg	
Zinc: . . . . .55 mg		Cholesterol: . . . . . . .269.67 mg	
Vitamin A: . . . . . . .1359.83 iu		Sodium: . . . . .36.67 mg	

Pot De Creme Ice Cream

½   cup water
1   six ounce package semi-sweet chocolate
3   egg yolks
1   four ounce carton frozen whipped topping,
       thawed

In a small saucepan heat water to boiling. Immediately pour over chocolate in blender container or food processor bowl. Cover and blend until chocolate is melted. Add egg yolks; cover and blend until thickened and smooth, stopping occasionally to scrape sides of blender. Remove mixture to a mixing bowl; fold dessert topping into chocolate mixture. Turn into a 9x5x3 inch loaf pan and freeze firm. Scoop into small balls or cut into squares to serve. Makes 6 servings.

Nutritional Analysis Per Serving:

Calories: 201	Vitamin C: . . . . .0 mg
Protein: . . . . .2.5 g	Thiamine: . . . . .02 mg
Carbohydrates: . . . . .18.33 g	Riboflavin: . . . . .05 mg
Fat: . . . . .15 g	Niacin: . . . . .15 mg
Phosphate: . . . . .81.33 mg	Calcium: . . . . .30.33 mg
Potassium: . . . . .100.5 mg	Iron: . . . . .1.17 mg
Zinc: . . . . .37 mg	Cholesterol: . . . . .120 mg
Vitamin A: . . . . .223.83 iu	Sodium: . . . . .6.5 mg

Apricot Banana Whip

1   16 ounce can apricot halves, drained
2   small ripe bananas, broken into 1 inch chunks
2   tablespoons lemon juice
3   packets of Equal®
2   egg whites at room temperature
    few grains of salt

Process apricots, bananas and lemon juice in blender or food processor until smooth. In the small bowl of an electric mixer, beat egg whites and salt at high speed until soft peaks form when beaters are lifted. Add Equal® and beat 1 to 2 minutes longer, until stiff peaks form. Gently fold in pureed fruit. Pour into 6 parfait glasses or dessert dishes. Chill 1 hour or overnight. Makes 6 servings.

Nutritional Analysis Per Serving:

Calories: 69	Vitamin C: . . . . .6.83 mg
Protein: . . . . .1.67 g	Thiamine: . . . . .03 mg
Carbohydrates: . . . . .16.83 g	Riboflavin: . . . . .05 mg
Fat: . . . . .17 g	Niacin: . . . . .4 mg
Phosphate: . . . . .15.67 mg	Calcium: . . . . .8.33 mg
Potassium: . . . . .231 mg	Iron: . . . . .35 mg
Zinc: . . . . .1 mg	Cholesterol: . . . . .0 mg
Vitamin A: . . . . .757.17 iu	Sodium: . . . . .15.33 mg

Tofu Smoothie

½   cup tofu
1   small banana
1   teaspoon lemon juice
1   tablespoon honey
½   cup yogurt
      ice

Blend together the tofu, banana, lemon juice, honey, ice and yogurt; adding water to thin, if necessary. Blend until smooth. Serve in a tall, frosted glass. Dust the top with cinnamon. (May use other fruit instead of banana.) Makes 2 servings.

Nutritional Analysis Per Serving:

Calories:	150	Vitamin C:	6.5 mg
Protein:	8.5 g	Thiamine:	1 mg
Carbohydrates:	25.5 g	Riboflavin:	2 mg
Fat:	2.5 g	Niacin:	5 mg
Phosphate:	184 mg	Calcium:	202.5 mg
Potassium:	365.5 mg	Iron:	1.6 mg
Zinc:	1.15 mg	Cholesterol:	1 mg
Vitamin A:	95 iu	Sodium:	52 mg

Pastel Whip

1   3 ounce box gelatin dessert, any flavor
1   cup boiling water
2   cups ice cubes
1   cup plain lowfat yogurt
½   teaspoon vanilla

Dissolve gelatin in boiling water. Add ice cubes and stir constantly until gelatin begins to thicken, 3 to 5 minutes. Remove any unmelted ice cubes. Add yogurt and vanilla and beat with rotary beater until light and fluffy pour into serving dishes and chill until set. Makes 4 servings.

Nutritional Analysis Per Serving:

Calories:	105.25	Vitamin C:	.5 mg
Protein:	21.75 g	Thiamine:	.03 mg
Carbohydrates:	4.75 g	Riboflavin:	.15 mg
Fat:	.25 g	Niacin:	.05 mg
Phosphate:	96 mg	Calcium:	124 mg
Potassium:	160.75 mg	Iron:	.05 mg
Zinc:	.65 mg	Cholesterol:	1 mg
Vitamin A:	.43 iu	Sodium:	66.25 mg

Pineapple-Cheese Casserole

20	ounce can crushed pineapple
½	cup honey
3	tablespoons flour
1	cup cheddar cheese, shredded
¼	cup margarine, melted
½	cup cracker crumbs

Drain pineapple, reserving 3 tablespoons juice. Mix honey, flour and reserved juice in bowl. Stir in pineapple and cheese. Place pineapple mixture in lightly greased casserole. Mix butter and cracker crumbs and sprinkle on top. Bake at 350 degrees for 30 minutes. Makes 6 servings.

Nutritional Analysis Per Serving:

Calories: 354	Vitamin C: .... 7.67 mg
Protein: .... 6.17 g	Thiamine: .... .15 mg
Carbohydrates: ..... 52.17 g	Riboflavin: .... .15 mg
Fat: .... 14.83 g	Niacin: .... .83 mg
Phosphate: .... 115.33 mg	Calcium: .... 153.83 mg
Potassium: .... 151 mg	Iron: .... 1.05 mg
Zinc: .... .78 mg	Cholesterol: .... 19.67 mg
Vitamin A: .... 566.67 iu	Sodium: .... 286 mg

Cranberry-Cheese Pie

1	15 ounce can sweetened condensed milk
⅓	cup lemon juice
½	teaspoon vanilla
1	8 ounce package cream sauce
1	16 ounce can whole cranberry sauce
1	9 inch vanilla wafer crust
1	cup chilled whipped cream

Put milk, lemon juice, vanilla, cheese and cranberry sauce in blender; blend until smooth. Spoon into crust. Freeze until firm. Remove from freezer ten minutes before serving. Top with whipped cream. Makes 6 servings.

Nutritional Analysis Per Serving:

Calories:...........756.5	Vitamin C:..........10.5 mg
Protein:..........12.33 g	Thiamine:...........12 mg
Carbohydrates:....109.17 g	Riboflavin:..........55 mg
Fat:...............32.5 g	Niacin:..............45 mg
Phosphate:.......327.17 mg	Calcium:..........334.83 mg
Potassium:........527.5 mg	Iron:...............1.07 mg
Zinc:..............1.33 mg	Cholesterol:........77.17 mg
Vitamin A:.......1233.17 iu	Sodium:............429 mg

Avocado Dessert

2   large avocados
18   packets of Equal®
¼   cup heavy cream
¼   cup lime juice
¼   teaspoon salt

Add avocados, Equal® , cream, lime juice and salt to food processor or blender. Process until smooth. Pour into individual molds and chill for 4 hours. Makes 4 servings.

Nutritional Analysis Per Serving:

Calories:...........315.5	Vitamin C: ....23.25 mg
Protein: ....3.5 g	Thiamine: .... .15 mg
Carbohydrates: .....14.75 g	Riboflavin:........... .3 mg
Fat:...............29.75 g	Niacin: ....2.27 mg
Phosphate: ....70.75 mg	Calcium:...........26.25 mg
Potassium:........884.25 mg	Iron:............... .87 mg
Zinc:............... .62 mg	Cholesterol:.........20.5 mg
Vitamin A: ....633.25 iu	Sodium: ....156.75 mg

Fruit Filling Cake

2   21 ounce cans fruit pie filling
1   box yellow cake mix
1   cup butter, melted

Layer pie filling, cake mix and butter in greased baking pan. Bake at 350 degrees for 50 minutes. Serve topped with ice cream. Makes 10 servings.

Nutritional Analysis Per Serving:

Calories:	344.2	Vitamin C:	1.6 mg
Protein:	2.4 g	Thiamine:	.08 mg
Carbohydrates:	33 g	Riboflavin:	.09 mg
Fat:	23.4 g	Niacin:	.68 mg
Phosphate:	54.9 mg	Calcium:	40.5 mg
Potassium:	101.3 mg	Iron:	.62 mg
Zinc:	.2 mg	Cholesterol:	70.4 mg
Vitamin A:	782.9 iu	Sodium:	287.3 mg

Pineapple Cheese Dessert

1   package yellow cake mix
8   ounces cream cheese, room temperature
2   cups milk
1   3½ ounce box instant vanilla pudding
20   ounces drained crushed pineapple
1   12 ounce carton prepared whipped topping

Bake yellow cake mix according to package instructions in a 9x13 pan and let cool.

Place 2 cups of milk in mixing bowl and mix in the cream cheese and instant vanilla pudding. Use an electric beater to mix completely. Spread mixture over cake. Now over mixture spread drained crushed pineapple. Spread whipped topping over pineapple just before serving. Makes 8 servings.

Nutritional Analysis Per Serving:

Calories:	509.5	Vitamin C:	6.88 mg
Protein:	9.13 g	Thiamine:	.2 mg
Carbohydrates:	62.13 g	Riboflavin:	.36 mg
Fat:	26.13 g	Niacin:	1.04 mg
Phosphate:	204.75 mg	Calcium:	215 mg
Potassium:	333.63 mg	Iron:	1.2 mg
Zinc:	.85 mg	Cholesterol:	75.25 mg
Vitamin A:	886 iu	Sodium:	287.25 mg

Apricot Whip

1   pound package dried apricots
1   teaspoon orange juice
¼   cup honey
3   egg whites

In a saucepan slowly heat apricots, orange juice and honey. Place mixture in blender and blend until smooth. Beat egg whites until stiff and fold into apricot mixture. Refrigerate and serve chilled. Makes 4 servings.

Nutritional Analysis Per Serving:

Calories: 179	Vitamin C: . . . . .5 mg
Protein: . . . . .4.25 g	Thiamine: . . . . .0 mg
Carbohydrates: . . . . .44.25 g	Riboflavin: . . . . .12 mg
Fat: . . . . .25 g	Niacin: . . . . .1.4 mg
Phosphate: . . . . .46.75 mg	Calcium: . . . . .30.25 mg
Potassium: . . . . .432 mg	Iron: . . . . .2.3 mg
Zinc: . . . . .32 mg	Cholesterol: . . . . .0 mg
Vitamin A: . . . . .4360 iu	Sodium: . . . . .44.5 mg

INDEX

Beverages
Aids:

Fruit:

Punch:

Shakes:

Soups

Main Dishes

Beef:

Chicken:

Eggs and Cheese:

Lamb:

Pork:

Seafood:

Turkey:

Vegetables

Asparagus:

Sweet Potato:

Squash:

Tomato:

Zucchini:

Desserts

Custard:

Fruit:

Ice:

Ice Cream:

Pudding:

Sherbet:

Whip:

NOTES

NOTES

NOTES

NOTES

NOTES

Use these postcards to order extra copies of
the **Non-Chew Cookbook** for your friends
and to keep your own cookbook up-to-date.

- -

Please add my name

To your mailing list to inform me
of future updates of Non-Chew Cookbook

Name _____
     (PRINT OR TYPE)
Address _____
            (STREET ADDRESS ONLY)
City_____ State_____ Zip_____

- -

Orders: Toll Free 1-800-843-2409

Please rush me _____ copies of the **Non-Chew Cookbook.**

1-9 Books	$14.95 each	10 or more books
Plus	$ 2.50 postage & handling	$10.47 each
		30% discount
	$17.45 each	(We pay postage)

Charge to my:

_____ VISA _____ Mastercard _____ Check or money order

Card # _____Exp. Date_____

Signature _____

Name _____
     (PRINT OR TYPE)
Address _____
            (STREET ADDRESS ONLY)
City_____ State_____ Zip_____